THE REPARATIVE MOTIF

IN CHILD AND ADULT THERAPY

Hugh Griffith Clegg

New York • Jason Aronson • *London*

Cover photo: Courtesy of the *British Medical Journal*.

Copyright © 1984 by Jason Aronson, Inc.

10 9 8 7 6 5 4 3 2 1

Library of Congress Cataloging in Publication Data

Clegg, Hugh Griffith.
  The reparative motif in child and adult therapy.

  Bibliography: p. 215.
  Includes index.
  1. Psychotherapy. 2. Healing. I. Title. [DNLM:
1. Emotions—In infancy and childhood. 2. Personality
development. 3. Psychoanalysis—In infancy and childhood.
4. Psychotherapy—In infancy and childhood. WS 105.5.P3
C624r]
RC480.5.C553 1984   616.89′14   84-2901
ISBN 0-87668-704-4

Manufactured in the United States of America.

I dedicate what follows
to my mother and late father,
and to my first professional "mother,"
Marie Singer, Ph.D., of Cambridge, England.

Contents

List of Figures   *ix*
Preface   *xi*
Introduction   1

1. THE DEVELOPMENT OF EXPRESSIVE
   PLAY THERAPY   11

   The Psychoanalytic Movement
   The Psychoanalytic Play Technique
   Lowenfeld's Expressive Play Technique
   Expressive Play and Symbolism
   Infant Development
   Contemporary Syntheses of Theories of Play
     and Development

2. A TOPOGRAPHICAL INTERPRETATION
   OF KLEINIAN THEORY   23

   The English School
   Content and Articulation of the Personality
   Individuation and the Onset of the Depressive Position

3. THE CONCEPT OF REPARATION   41

   Klein's Earliest Ideas
   The Beginning of Child Analysis in London
   First Ideas about Reparation
   Reparation as a Forerunner of Autonomy
   Splitting and Reparation
   Constitutionally Determined Emotional Dispositions
   The Balance of the Personality
   Transitional Regulating Mechanisms
   The Establishment of Internal Conflicts
   The Play Therapy Paradigm

4. THE CLINICAL APPROACH   55

   Exemplary Protocols
   Examples of Children's Expressive Play in Play Therapy

5.   THE SETTING   67

The Community
The Diagnostic Consultation

6.   THE FIRST CASE: JENNIFER   73

The Consultation Data
Presuppositions about the Child's Expressive Play
Play Sessions
Analysis of Jennifer's Play

7.   THE SECOND CASE: CHRISTINE   101

The Consultation Data
The Play Scenes
Analysis of the Play Sessions

8.   REPARATIVE CHANGE   119

Reflections of Development in the Play Themes
The Confluence of Danger and Love
Inferences vis-à-vis Reparation
The Changes in the Play Themes
Help from an Other
The Reparative Motif and Reparative Mechanisms
The Preoccupation of the Child by a Conflict
The Distorting Effects of Developmental Vicissitudes

9.   REPARATION IN THERAPY WITH
     AN ADULT   131

10. BEYOND COUNTERTRANSFERENCE:
     ACTIVITY IN THE MIND OF THE
     THERAPIST   155

Conscious Response
Countertransference
Autochthonous Thoughts and Fantasies

11. THE THERAPIST'S CONTRIBUTION
     IN THE REPARATIVE PROCESS   165

Indirect Therapeutic Influences
More Direct Influences

The Revival and Sharing of Primitive Fantasies
Therapeutic Intimacy and Distance
A Contrasting Technique
The True and the False Self
The Parallel with Somatic Immune Mechanisms

12. **REPARATION IN THE FAMILY CONSTELLATION**   181

13. **REPARATION THROUGH TRANSITIONAL PROCESSES**   197

The Professional Environment
Countertransference in Play Therapy and
    in Play Therapy Supervision

14. **PREVALENCE OF THE REPARATIVE MOTIF**   205

The Model Used
The Evolving Play Themes
Reparation in Play Therapy
Theoretical Foundations
Summary

References   *215*
Index   *221*

List of Figures

1. The variety of objects.   33
2. A field of various objects.   34
3. "Splitting" in operation.   34
4. Domination by bad objects.   35
5. Differential organization of good and bad objects.   35
6. Two individuals.   36
7. A part of a balanced personality.   37
8. An accident.   60
9. An articulated rescue scene.   61
10. David's town.   62
11. Crash of the century.   64
12. A mountain.   79
13. Hill with jewels on top.   82
14. Two palm trees.   105
15. An abandoned castle.   106
16. A prehistoric scene.   106
17. Hide-and-seek game.   107
18. Procession of animals.   107
19. Procession in context.   108
20. Complex scene.   109
21. "My hearts."   110
22. The house theme.   110
23. "Your house and mine."   111
24. Reparative scene.   112
25. A molecular analog.   128
26. Antigen–antibody reaction.   177
27. The influences on a child.   188

Preface

This book is about the psychological mechanism of reparation, the effort to restore damaged aspects of the self. Reparation is used in the maintenance of emotional equilibrium in the personality development of the child, and it continues to serve this function throughout adult life unless overwhelmed by traumata. I examine the mechanism by inferential reconstruction in the cases of children in whom it has failed and been restored through therapeutic intervention. I also describe an adult case in which one can observe the restoration of this reparative mechanism in the course of psychotherapy. The moment at which restoration of a functioning reparative mechanism occurs is marked by the emergence of a new and qualitatively different theme in both children's play and adults' associative trains: the reparative motif.

The model of the mind that I have employed and described is based on the English school of object relations psychoanalysis elaborated by Melanie Klein. Additionally, I have been influenced in the formulation of my theory by ideas taken from embryology and the physiological development of the individual, from genetics, and from the mechanisms of the immune system in the maintenance of physical health.

I have sought parallels between certain aspects of morphological development, organization, and the differentiation of function in somatic development with corresponding aspects of psychological development. In this respect I have looked at the patterning of a child's therapeutic play or of an adult's verbal associations as the mirror of internal organization and of the contents of the mind. Specifically, embryological development shows mechanisms in the physical formation of the organism, the morphology of the individual, that are designed to insure the integrity of developmental processes. At successive stages of development, structures differentiate progressively from an unformed matrix of cells according to an organizing principle. I have regarded personality development as similarly organized in a sequential way, allowing increasing diversity and sophistication in the repertoire of mechanisms that the individual uses to defend against the challenges of everyday life. Children's mental themes or motifs express the organization and direction of their emotions. In adult thinking, the complexity and articulation of the themes make the discernment of fundamental processes more difficult, but through analysis of unconscious determinants of the theme it is possible to view the mechanisms I am describing.

The significance of the reparative motif derives from theoretical aspects of Kleinian thinking as well as from clinical observations. The concept of reparation as it was described by Melanie Klein is extended in my work to predict the mechanisms that are crucial in the development of character structure and in the subsequent maintenance of the internal balance of the emotions: the confluence of love and hate within the overall architecture of the personality. I describe in detail clinical themes that allow inference to be drawn concerning the nature of reparation as a mechanism and the way in which psychotherapy acts to restore emotional health.

In order to address both theoretical and clinical issues systematically, I have divided the book into two parts. First, I reexamine Klein's ideas, with special reference to the concept of reparation: its function, mechanism, and incidence during personality development. I have reformulated Kleinian theory into a topographical model that lends itself readily to the understanding of play themes and adult associations as indicators of the content and articulation of the personality. Second, I apply these theoretical formulations to analyze the changing themes of successive therapy sessions with two children and one young woman. The themes show a discontinuity at the point where the balance of the emotions shifts: where the descent into the vortex of conflict and despair is arrested and is replaced by a more balanced admixture in which themes of safety, of being loved and able to love, and of being aggressive enough to defend oneself against life's insults are seen.

The themes I describe are well known in many art forms. The human quest, to suffer bravely, to love insistently, to hate when one must, and eventually to triumph in life by countenancing death are captured in the stories of many operas, dance pieces, and dramas. I particularly acknowledge "Errand into the Maze" performed by the Martha Graham Dance Company as influential in my thinking about the nature of the reparative motif.

These diverse influences on my thinking address one central concern, the central problem in psychotherapy: the mechanism of recovery. This theme echoes one of humanity's historically important concerns: the survival of and recovery from tragedy.

> *There is an errand into the maze of the heart's darkness in order to face and do battle with the Creature of Fear. There is the accomplishment of the errand, the instant of triumph, and the emergence from the dark.*
>
> —The Martha Graham Dance Foundation (1980)

Introduction

This study of the health-seeking processes seen in the child in play therapy has evolved over some 18 years since my interest in child analysis was kindled by Marie Singer in her short course of lectures at Cambridge University in the spring of 1967. Mrs. Singer had trained with Anna Freud at the Hampstead Clinic and discussed her work with me informally at her cottage in the Cambridgeshire countryside. Our somewhat general discussions on the nature of the child's mind left a curiosity in me that I was not fully aware of for some years.

Cambridge psychology was inclined toward the experimental, behavioral, and physiological branches of the science at that time, although a diverse range of lecturers from B. F. Skinner to R. D. Laing held forth from time to time. Martin P. Richards had returned from studying with T. G. R. Bower at Harvard to establish a research program in perinatal development at the Unit for Research into the Medical Applications of Psychology. He was interested in the influence of prenatal factors, medical interventions during delivery (such as anesthesia), and postnatal influences on the baby's development. Oliver Zangwill, Britain's foremost neuropsychologist and theoretician, allowed me to sit in while he conducted an examination of a child at the National Hospital in Queen's Square, London, and I recall thinking that his clinical sensitivity and gentleness with the child had a magical quality. Zangwill was (and still is) interested in the co-function of the brain and the psyche, and he led me to think in terms of neurological and psychological interdigitation. Zangwill also made the arrangements that enabled me to pursue my own interests, both during and after my studies at the Psychological Laboratory. I should also mention a short study that I made on the treatment of asthmatic children using behavior therapy (Moore 1965). A local physician, Dr. J. Sills, referred the children to me and supervised their medical care. In the course of this project, a number of children at once lost their asthma completely, some after many years of illness. Although everyone was initially delighted, as I followed up their remission some months and years later, I became aware of and was startled by dramatic family changes consequent on the successful treatment of the child's asthma. I knew from that time that family systems are profoundly interdependent and that one disturbs the status quo at substantial risk of unpredictable "side" effects.

Two of my undergraduate contemporaries at Cambridge influenced me through their friendship and their ideas. Philip Evans (now at the Northeast London University) was a more dyed-in-the-wool Freudian and vigorous enthusiast for psychoanalysis than I was at that time, and he brought me to understand concepts I had practically given up on ever understanding—partly through his enthusiasm and partly through his incisive intellect. Sigurd Reimers, destined for a career in the field of social work similar to mine in psychology, never failed to remind me of the importance of family history and of family processes to the child. I would attempt to rebut his convincing arguments with my own ideas about the influence of the child on the development of the family and on the parents as individuals. My thinking goes back and forth on these issues, and the present study exemplifies some of my attempts to come to an understanding of the co-influence of child and parent.

One small study I had made concerned the relation between primary suggestibility (hypnotizability) and another personality variable, field dependence. In the course of this study, I came across several deeply suggestible ("somnambulistic") subjects from whom I learned something about the manifestations of repression, denial, rationalization, and other mechanisms of defense.

GRADUATE CLINICAL EXPERIENCES

My next clinical training was at the University of Aberdeen as part of a course designed to introduce analytic psychotherapy to psychiatrists. The course was quite broad in scope, with a variety of orientations, but there was a distinct depth-psychology and object relations emphasis. The patients I saw had Kleinian dreams and associations, used transitional objects (including myself) in their therapy, and generally were comprehensible to me through my neophyte eyes as a beginning student of object relations theory. The course favored the "Middle School" of object relations theorists: Guntrip, Balint, Fairbairn, Winnicott, Rochlin, Mahler, et al. It was not until later that I could begin to understand Melanie Klein and her more orthodox followers; for example, Marion Milner.

From this irresistible introduction to object relationships, it was perhaps inevitable that I should become a student of the function and nature of transitional objects, both as developmental phenomena and as a vital force in the treatment of emotional distress. I thought of ideas, words, dreams, and of course play as transitional phenomena. I also thought of the many ways in which therapists themselves are used in this connection, as communicators between one part of the patient's mind and another. This idea is used not only in psychotherapy, but in general medicine (Balint 1957) and in other forms of therapy, such as in art therapy or the use of art in psychotherapy.

A fellow trainee, Dr. John Birtchnell, made a dramatic film (1970) showing the way in which a patient's recovery in the course of expressive psychotherapy was documented in the vivid paintings the patient had produced. The idea of tracing a patient's fantasy productions through art is not new, but Birtchnell brought a scientific and psychoanalytic perspicacity to his attempts to formulate the dynamic significance of the patient's art. Birtchnell (1973) laid the basis for some of the methods in this study:

> The present study is an attempt to reveal the psychopathology expressed in the pictures and to show the relationship between this psychopathology and the patient's symptoms, current circumstances, and preceding history. How, then, can the author be sure that his interpretations of these pictures were in fact the ideas the patient was trying to express? There is the very real danger that the author may have read into them some of his own personal fantasies.
>
> The method of analysis adopted, insofar as the author was aware of it, was first to attempt to establish connections between the situations within the pictures and those within the patient's real life. Details of

his past life, present situation, and clinical state were available from the case record. Second, the author tried to discover within the pictures internal consistencies in terms of recurrence of themes, motifs, shapes, and so on. An object in a particular place on one sheet of paper became transformed into a different, though related, object on another. A hypothesis suggested by one picture could be supported or refuted by other pictures in the series. The interpretations finally arrived at were those that best fitted the content of the majority of the pictures and that were most meaningful in terms of the patient's history and present life-situation.

During the course of his stay the patient produced approximately 60 pictures. It is not possible to discuss here the content of all of them; instead an analysis of seven of the most significant ones will be undertaken. (p. 212)

I will use some of Birtchnell's approaches in my analysis of the material in the child's play productions.

This study can be traced back in its earliest conceptions to some 15 years ago, when I saw my first child in play therapy. I had already some understanding of elementary principles of expressive psychotherapy, and my own analysis was in its second year. However, I had little idea what "to do" as a play therapist. My adult supervisor, Dr. Richard Mackie, had already led me to understand the great dangers of diminishing my own anxieties by saying something or doing something in the treatment of adults: this is no more than the injunction on acting-out the countertransference, which we generally observe. "Don't just do something, sit there," Mackie would remind me.

Therefore, in the beginning of my treatment of this first child, I at the least tried to fulfill the mandate of the Hippocratic injunction: *primum non nocere.* My notion of following this role was to allow and observe the child's play in which this boy of 8 years made a World scene whose meaning escaped my unpracticed eyes completely. I carefully recorded the child's play as it developed and what the child told me about the scene. I mulled it over in my mind, both during and after the session. For the rest of the day, I would find the scene returning to my mind in every unguarded moment and often when I was in the middle of something else. It was not that my concentration was defective but rather that some elements of the play had made a dramatic emotional impact on me and were preoccupying some part of my mind. That night I dreamed not about the child himself, but about the World he had made. The scene came alive in my dreams in a seemingly meaningful way, but on awakening, the meaning had again slipped away from me.

I continued not to "understand" this child for many weeks, during which time he was becoming more relaxed and affectionate at home and at school while his play scenes with me became more and more depraved. I was worrying more while he was worrying less. As the scenes proceeded into increasingly disorganized scenes of mass destruction, I found myself trying to think of perceptive interpretations, struggling more arduously to comprehend the scenes and becoming concerned that I might indeed be damaging the child through my ignorance or inexperience. To my own amazement, the child's mother continued to report favorable improvements in his disposition to the social worker with whom I was sharing the case. (In the orthodox child guidance model, I saw the child, she the parents, and we met to discuss the treatment and to be supervised.) The child was clearly more flexible, alert, and contented in his real world as his play world came to contain more and more of his distress and anger.

Quite suddenly, and again without classical interpretation on my part, the play themes after five or six months changed into much more benign and organized scenes. I would feel very different after these sessions compared with the early ones, as if a great burden had been lifted from both the child and myself. I came to feel some weeks later that the therapy was losing its significance for the child, and I ended treatment some two months after this transition occurred.

This account is greatly simplified and designed to show the origins of my curiosity about what, if anything, I had done to help this child. Although I have not described this case in depth, it was clear that, either spontaneously or through my intervention, the child had recovered from incapacitating anxieties and school phobia. A two-year follow-up showed that his progress was sustained.

When I would try to believe that the child had undergone some kind of spontaneous remission in my presence, I would be reminded of the sense of intense mental preoccupation with his play in myself. I should also mention that I undoubtedly could not have sustained my own courage in the treatment hours had it not been for the supervision I received from Dr. Ian Lowit, whom I saw hourly for each hour I saw the child. He appeared to understand the child's and my struggles, even though I did not.

EARLY PROFESSIONAL WORK

I was at that time coming to think of some child-directed, unconscious therapeutic process, which child and therapist embark on together, as a process in which the child holds the tiller and the throttle. After learning a little of Margaret Lowenfeld's techniques from Lowit and visiting her clinic in London, I left Aberdeen to work at the University of Sussex Health Center, directed by Anthony Ryle. Ryle's studies included the epidemiology of students' mental health and problems, and he was vigorously combining the psychological and physical aspects of medicine as a health-giving influence in the university community. Twice-weekly case conferences were conducted by Dr. F. Shadforth, who was able to bring Klein's ideas to life and to clarify them in cogent and clinically helpful ways. I commuted to London each week to study at the Institute for Group Analysis, which consisted of a number of group analytic practitioners in the tradition of Bion, Foulkes, Ezriel, and (more recently) Yalom. Dana Breen was a research psychologist and psychotherapist at the University Health Service, and her distinguished research into the woman's view of herself at the time of the birth of a first child has contributed to my recent thinking in ways that are reflected in this study (see, for example, Breen 1975).

I wanted an opportunity to observe the antecedents of adolescent personality processes, and I am grateful to Dr. Sidney Cohen of the Youth Psychotherapy Center of the Bryn Mawr Hospital, Bryn Mawr, Pennsylvania, who passed on my letter of inquiry to him to

Dr. Gunther Abraham of the Devereaux Foundation in Devon, Pennsylvania. Dr. Abraham offered me a position as a psychologist working with 11- to 16-year-olds and with 5- to 12-year-olds in two units of the Devereaux Foundation, a residential treatment center for children. Dr. Yvonne Agazarian generously supervised me, and Dr. James Pearson shared his clinical acumen and therapeutic wisdom with me. Numerous interns whom I taught challenged all of my assumptions.

One intern with whom I worked is worthy of special mention for her diligence and perspicacity. Ms. Maya Brutten and I conducted a thrice-weekly analytic group for the most severely disturbed adolescents, a group that I remember as one of the most demanding clinical experiences I have ever undertaken.

The group met every Monday, Wednesday, and Friday for a year. The Friday sessions were marked by the "weekend effect," namely a sense of increased deprivation, depression, and muted rage. (This effect also includes the intensified, exaggerated, oral-dependent neediness bordering on emptiness, usually coupled with masked rage, that occurs when the regular schedule of analytic sessions is interrupted by the weekend.) On one occasion, responding to this effect (which both of us found quite harrowing), Maya stayed up to the small hours of the night baking cookies to offer the children the next day. When the group assembled, they fought briefly over the cookies before consuming them voraciously. They did not, however, say a word more about the cookies, neither to wonder where they had come from nor, of course, to evince any gratitude. Klein's study of envy and gratitude (1957) amply shows the dynamic imperative for the absence of gratitude. In fact, the group had taken the cookies as a sign of how much they had missed in life, and they remained angry, sullen, and resentful for almost two weeks.

Leonard Green and Robert Young, clinical administrators at separate Devereaux units, made it possible for me to work with very young children and allowed me time to take graduate courses in genetics and embryology at a nearby private university. I was also able to hear the "New American School" of object relations from such pioneers as Arlow, Kernberg, Kohut, and others at the Albert Einstein Medical Center in Philadelphia and at the Philadelphia Psychoanalytic Society and Association. Barbara Hirsch, an inspired child therapist and family social worker, contributed in many ways to my ability to work creatively with very young children and their families. It was during my work with her that I first became aware that therapeutic success depended crucially on the respect of the child's parents for me (even though this was a residential center, and the parents would see me infrequently) and on the child's and my ability to descend together to the frightening depths of the pain-filled domains of the child's fantasy life.

One young woman, Diane (a pseudonym), who was quite paralyzed by fear, brought her childhood doll when she talked to me about the subjects that she felt too shy to tell me about. This young woman left a particularly deep impression on me, not only in the depth of the love we held for one another but also because of the almost magical ability she had to show me, in vivid and unforgettable ways, the unfolding of her own treatment before my very eyes. Because she was too shy to talk about herself, and because discursive reasoning was far removed from the emotional depths of her anguish, Diane thus brought in her childhood rag doll (whose real name I also cannot disclose; I will call the doll "Muffie"). Muffie had been with Diane since her infancy; her insides were regularly replaced with kapok, and her body needed refabrication every seven or eight years. But the essence of Muffie continued unchanged.

Diane expressed to me many complex emotional ideas through her stories about Muffie. It became clear to me that Muffie was a transitional (going between) object in the fullest sense: transitional between Diane and myself, between Diane's present and her past, but most important, between one part of Diane and another. The investment of this bridge represented for Diane (and became her solution to) a life-or-death dilemma, the dilemma of whether to remain locked up inside a shell of suspicious detachment or whether to allow herself to join in the risky business of day-to-day relationships.

MORE RECENT INTERESTS

In Berkeley I have traced my interest further back in the age range of children to infancy, but most of my clinical work over the last five years has been with children in the 3- to 7-year-old age group, of whom I have seen about a hundred once or twice weekly in outpatient play therapy. I have also been a weekly consultant to a dozen other child therapists in this area, through whose work I have been able to study a substantial number of other children in treatment, though somewhat less fully than the children I have seen myself.

A special word of gratitude goes to the parents who brought their children to me, to the children themselves, and to my clinical students who, as Winnicott says, "have paid to teach me." As a collaborator and friend, Barbara Feldmar, in particular, has enabled me to see patterns of recovery in many children and has sometimes given me the courage to go on. Mervin Freedman helped me to express the ideas herein and convinced me to develop them further.

1
The Development of
Expressive Play Therapy

THE PSYCHOANALYTIC MOVEMENT

Psychoanalysis has provided a heuristic technique that is capable of probing some of the complexities of the human personality. The modern understanding of play as an expressive medium that manifests a child's personality grew out of Freud's elucidation of the underlying determinants of the emotional dynamics at different stages of the child's development.

Freud (1895) had attempted to fathom the causes of hysterical states through hypnotic and, later, free association and dream analysis avenues. His search for what lay beyond the veils of amnesia led him to formulate the mechanism of repression and to the discovery of infantile sexuality. Of particular relevance to this study was Freud's description, echoing that of Robert Carter (1853), of the *idée fixe*—a specific pathogenic motif that, although repressed, continued its attack on the ego. These lost memories emerged in the patients' dreams and verbal associations, permitting inferential reconstruction of the initial cause of the hysterical phenomenon.

The formulation of models for the mechanism of therapeutic change in the personality goes back to the beginning of psychoanalysis. The development of the economic model of personality regulation by Freud allowed delineations of pathological processes (such as widespread repression) and of the direction that therapeutic change might take. Freud and Breuer (1895) began by using hypnotic abreaction or catharsis to purge the psyche of repressed sexual energy. This technique gave way to the more gradual approach of free association and the analysis of dreams. Catharsis and insight were fostered by interpretations of the repressed affect

13

and later by development of the understanding of defense mechanisms, of resistance in the transference, and of the transference itself. The therapeutic effects were thought to come from both the liberation of trapped affect and the integration of a conscious understanding of the infantile origins of this exaggerated affect in the transference.

It was found that there are points of discontinuity in psychoanalysis when a sudden dawning of insight, a crystallization of many preconscious ideas, takes place in the patient's mind. This critical event is brought about, or at any rate released from the unconscious, by a crucial therapeutic intervention, the mutative interpretation. Classical analysis emphasizes the critical significance of the mutative interpretation. (This study will seek equivalents of the mutative interpretation in the autochthonous fantasies of children in play therapy.) Early rebels in the psychoanalytic movement, such as Ferenczi (1924), suggested that the analyst's emotional expressivity might also be an important agent of therapeutic change.

The hypothetico-deductive model developed by Freud was based on the inferential reconstruction of childhood experience through analysis of adult memories, free associations, and dreams, and also in the revival of early relationship patterns in characteristic transference attitudes (Home 1971). This model was used in attempts to formulate childhood neurotic presentations dynamically, as in the case of "Little Hans" (Freud 1909), although Hans himself was never seen in treatment. Rather, Freud's interpretations were conveyed to him by his father who consulted Freud. It was not until some years later that analytic techniques were used directly in the treatment of children.

THE PSYCHOANALYTIC PLAY TECHNIQUE

Hug-Hellmuth (1921) and Klein (1921) had analyzed children using verbal utterances and play themes as the child's equivalent of the adult tools, free association, and remembering. Klein had studied with Ferenczi in Vienna before he began to rebel against the mainstream of classical analysis. She had subsequently moved to Berlin to study with and to be analyzed by Abraham, who was also intensely interested in studying children. Only eight months after Klein began her analysis with Abraham, he died quite suddenly, leaving her to pioneer the psychoanalysis of children with the perspicacity and temerity for which she is now well known. Klein (1932) was to write of Abraham: "He said, in words I shall never forget: 'The future of psychoanalysis lies in play technique.' My theoretical conclusions are a natural development of his own discoveries" (p. xi).

Ernest Jones had made himself an advocate of child analysis in England, and it was at his invitation that Klein first gave a series of lectures at the British Psychoanalytic Society in 1925. "I knew I was securing an extremely valuable recruit," Jones (1948) wrote, "but I had no idea what a commotion this would create" (p. 337).

Klein (1932) herself pointed out: "The study of the mind of the small child taught me certain facts which seemed strange at first sight" (p. xi). These facts were met with incredulity by the analysts in London at the 1925 meetings, but within five years Klein became a central figure in the British Psychoanalytic Society.

Anna Freud represented another method of child analysis. She also had modified classical technique and had come to the opinion that children do not develop a transference neurosis. (Transference refers to the revival in the therapeutic relationship of infantile remnants of the parent-child relationship, generally seen as misattributions to the therapist or as exaggerated emotional reactions in the therapeutic situation.) She felt that the child's mechanisms of defense were not so rigidly formed as those of the adult. She thought that the young child's ego still lives in accordance with the pleasure principle and that the child is "too weak to oppose the outside world actively" (A. Freud 1927, p. 49). She had been influenced by Aichorn's approaches with "wayward youth" (1935) and by Bernfeld who, informed by his experiences in homes for derelict children, first explored the limits of education (1929). Miss Freud formulated her own approach to the treatment of children, reflecting her interest in integrating the intellectual, somatic, and emotional influences in the child's personality and disposition to the world.

LOWENFELD'S EXPRESSIVE PLAY TECHNIQUE

Independently of the psychoanalytic movement, although perhaps influenced by it in ways that have not been acknowledged, Margaret Lowenfeld, a London pediatrician, developed a system of treating children with emotional difficulties through sand play: the World technique (1950). This work was contemporaneous with that of Klein and A. Freud in the mid-twenties. Lowenfeld had read H. G. Wells's *Floor Games* (1912), in which he described a type of play that his two sons found especially compelling. One room of Wells's house had been set aside for the "floor games." Shelves around the walls had models of almost every aspect of the real world. There were papier-mâché mountains, tunnels, bridges, vehicles, animals, people, buildings, and trees in great variety and profusion. In Wells's presence but without his intervention, his sons constructed imaginary scenes including magical islands, kingdoms, and countries. Lowenfeld found this a valuable expressive technique for the children with whom she was working.

One child moved the game from the floor to the sand tray that Lowenfeld had in her office for sand and water play. He molded the sand, making roads and hillsides that were elaborated with miniatures taken from the floor game. At the end of his creation, he exclaimed, "See, I have created a whole world!" (personal communication). From that moment (in 1928), Lowenfeld's technique became known as the World technique. Children appear to have a spontaneous knowledge of this form of play. It is not unusual for a child to enter the playroom for the first time and begin constructing a World with no instruction whatever on the part of the therapist.

Lowenfeld opened The Children's Clinic in North Kensington, London, in 1928. The clinic had many features in addition to Lowenfeld's Mosaic and World techniques. One member of her staff was a musician and another a dancer, their contributions previewing the modern disciplines of music and dance therapy. In 1937 the clinic received a bequest of money and moved to a house in which Robert Browning had once lived. At this time new dimensions were added to Lowenfeld's approaches to children. These included several experimental services:

(a) *Gynecological help to mothers.* It was found that minor gynecological disorders often lay at the root of the mother's fatigue and depression and interfered with the correct handling of her children.

(b) *Playroom equipment.* A carpenter's bench with tools was added to the equipment. The children's use of this not only confirmed the well-known fact that this type of activity can canalise aggressive and destructive feelings but also served as an outlet for blocked surplus energy.

(c) *Water.* It was at that time that workers first became aware of the value of water in therapy.

(d) *Garden.* The fact that a well-cultivated garden was available behind the house brought to light the excitement awakened in many of these London children by the simplest facts of growing seeds and flowering plants.

(e) *Records.* Case Sheets were designed in which each section of the work was filed separately and included in a simple folder. These with certain improvements are still in use and serve as a basis for further research.

(f) *Training.* As there existed no trained nonmedical psychotherapists at the time of the founding of the Children's Clinic, an elementary form of training for all the nonmedical workers at the clinic had already been devised. This was now developed into a formal three years' Training Course.

At the same time the title "The Children's Clinic" was changed to "The Institute of Child Psychology." (Lowenfeld 1969, p. 7)

Lowenfeld used the neutral therapeutic stance, a supportive but nonintrusive presence, in an attempt to create a "safe and free space" in which children could express their fantasies. Lowenfeld (1950) emphasized that "it is essential for the proper understanding of the nature and use of this technique [the World technique] that no interpretation be given by the therapist to the child. No object is to be taken at its face value, but careful inquiry is made of the child as to what exactly each object is to be recorded as being" (p. 327).

The purpose of this emphasis was to further the exploration of the hitherto unknown aspects of the child's inner experience, to find a means through which direct contact could be made with the inner experience of children. Lowenfeld was interested in the children's sensory and proprioceptive experience, their thoughts about them, and the affect that arises in response to the meanings that children impute to this aspect of their experience. This triad is known as a "cluster." It will be seen later in the theoretical discussion that the cluster corresponds closely to the nature of an object in Kleinian object relations theory.

Lowenfeld also described the difference in the way a child thinks as compared to an adult: A child does not think linearly; rather, thought, feeling, concept, and memory are inextricably interwoven. A child's thought is fluid, and movement can take place on several planes at once. This is, of course, what we would now describe as the nondiscursive reasoning of the child. Sand play has elements of touch and sensation that, added to sight, trigger deep aspects of the personality, and these emerge for expression in the World. The wide selection of miniatures provides a structured, "safe but free" way to translate these inner imaginings or memories into a scene.

Lowenfeld presented her ideas to the British Psychological Society in 1938 before an audience that included Klein and Winnicott. (Winnicott, also a pediatrician, was to rise to great prominence in the field of child psychiatry.) Lowenfeld illustrated her talk with lantern slides of children's Worlds. "When I had recovered from the lantern slides," Winnicott said to Lowenfeld, "I wondered what the purpose of this work could possibly be" (Lowenfeld 1938, p. 96). Klein suggested that Lowenfeld had borrowed from her (Klein's) work without admitting her debt to psychoanalysis, and that Lowenfeld was "discovering" phenomena long familiar to the psychoanalysts. Lowenfeld replied with her view that psychoanalysts foisted their dogma on unsuspecting children, applying the same rigid ideas to every child, regardless of their individual differences (e.g., see Lowenfeld 1969).

This historic meeting drove Lowenfeld and the Kleinians in divergent directions, in spite of the consonance that can, in retrospect, be seen in both technical and pragmatic aspects of their work.

Lowenfeld published little and seemed not to want to associate herself in any way with a metapsychology of the therapeutic process. The strikingly atheoretical nature of her play technique is illustrated in a work published posthumously (1979) under her name. The particular advantage that Lowenfeld's technique offers in this study is its lack of overt influence on the child, influence slanted in a particular theoretical direction. The meticulously detailed recordings of the child's play that Lowenfeld insisted on will be subjected to analysis, using predicates derived from an extension of Kleinian theory. The study thus attempts to reap the benefits to knowledge of bringing together two schools of thought that have been separated since 1938.

EXPRESSIVE PLAY AND SYMBOLISM

Kalff (1946), a Jungian analyst, studied with Lowenfeld and introduced sand play into the repertoire of Jungian child and adult treatment. Both her written work and a film she made to demonstrate her practice with children present illustrations of play therapy without making a link with theoretical propositions about the therapeutic mechanism.

Sechehaye (1950, 1956) devised a form of play therapy in the treatment of an adolescent schizophrenic girl that was then retrospectively linked with classical Freudian theory. This very important and original contribution, seemingly conceived out of desperation for the fate of this one patient, showed the possibility of the symbolic re-creation by the patient of unfulfilled infantile needs and of the satisfaction of these needs by a shared effort of the therapist and the patient. Sechehaye thus laid the groundwork for the idea that, in play, patients can devise a way to present the problem they experience intrapsychically to the therapist and can create a symbolic way for the problem to be solved.

Madeline Rambert (1949) had analyzed children systematically, using drawing as the child's principal expressive medium. Her records clearly show the emergence of reparative themes, and although Rambert herself does not describe the common changes in theme of the children's drawings, it seems that she probably was aware of them. Rambert does, however, show the pathognomonic properties of the drawings. And she shows the close parallel between the theme of the drawings and the child's personality on the one hand, and the style or organization of the drawings and the child's character structure on the other.

Rambert also showed the link between play themes and the child's dream life and described techniques for beginning to understand the child's "picture language." Rambert also described aspects of play and drawing therapy that appear in this study—in particular, the ability of the child to "lead the therapist into the deep layers of his personality" (p. 239) if the therapist is both able to follow and able to understand the child's symbolic communication.

Axline (1947) and Moustakas (1953) represent a contemporary school of play therapy in which historical antecedence is acknowledged as a formative influence on the personality, but emphasis is placed on current or earlier "reality" rather than on the psychological distortions of reality present in the mind of the child. Axline describes her work in painstaking detail, but the reader is left to infer depth-psychological derivatives of the mechanism of change.

Klein (1955) described her technique in treating children through "play analysis," but this paper was more general and included only fragments of clinical illustrations from several cases. In spite of her own formulation of reparation, Klein failed to illustrate this concept in an expository way in the themes of children in play therapy. In particular, she did not show in what ways reparative themes differ from other themes in the course of the child's treatment.

Smolen (1959) considered the nonverbal aspects of play therapy. His paper laid down some of the principles for understanding the child's communication through monitoring of the countertransference and the therapist's fantasies during the play. His observations give an important insight into some of the therapeutic processes occurring during the use of Lowenfeld's technique.

INFANT DEVELOPMENT

During the period 1951–1970, Bowlby was studying the reactions of infants to the loss of maternal care. His studies were part of a World Health Organization study of reactions to maternal deprivation. Through meticulously controlled studies, Bowlby (1969, 1973) showed the effects of the vicissitudes of early care on the child's personality development. Bowlby's work allows links to be made between observed developmental phenomena and the predictions of emotional processes made from psychoanalytic theory.

Fraiberg (1959) also described the consonance between early child-parent observations and the predictions derived from psychoanalytic theory. Fraiberg went on to devise a type of co-therapy for babies and their mothers in which she restores the child-mother interaction through a restoration of the mother's sense of her own nurturance.

Nagera (1966) defined various categories of infantile disturbance; in his view, there is a phase of development in which "all the neurotic conflicts and developmental shortcomings" come together into a single unit of organization "of the highest economic significance" (p. 24). Nagera sees the overcoming of this nexus as an essential turning point in human development, as the ultimate test of the ego's growing synthetic and integrative functions. Although couched in Freudian terms (of the "phallic-oedipal" phase), this description fits well the idea of a specific phase during which a major restorative leap must occur in order for development to progress adequately. I will return to this idea, both in the consideration of Klein's theories and in the analysis of the data of the study.

CONTEMPORARY SYNTHESES OF THEORIES OF PLAY AND DEVELOPMENT

Winnicott, widely regarded as the foremost authority on play therapy in the Kleinian tradition, published (between 1931 and his death in 1971) many works on the mental development of the child (several works have appeared posthumously). Of great importance to this study is his work on the role of the "transitional object" (1953), both initially in helping the child survive frightening or anger-inducing experiences and subsequently in the maintenance of resilience in the personality. It will be seen that the reparative motif is itself a form of transitional object of transcendent influence. In *The Piggle* (1977) Winnicott presents case material that allows an independent assessment of the reparative motif.

Nevertheless, much of Winnicott's style is so far from his or the reader's consciousness that his therapeutic technique appears almost magical, and the therapeutic process remains something of a mystery. His theoretical papers, however, do allow inference as to his ideas about the nature of therapeutic change, although this specific theme is not directly addressed.

Cooper and Wanerman (1977) described the modern school of play therapy with its developmental emphasis. These ideas, some of which will be presented in the next chapter (namely, the regressive recapitulation in play of early conflicts or deprivations), contain many of the features that give the context of the material of the present study. The essence of the study, the reparative motif, is most closely approached in the literature by Bloch (1979), who reports on the evolution of a reparative theme in a child's play. Bloch describes this theme as a defensive fantasy, but it is clear that she appreciates the ego-syntonic and central nature of this defensive operation.

2

A Topographical
Interpretation of
Kleinian Theory

The biological and physical sciences have made dramatic progress in this century, not only in the acquisition of knowledge but also in the development of a diverse range of paradigm-building techniques. These techniques permit the organization of facts into new heuristic models. As new discoveries are made, putative theoretical models can be created within the limits of Occam's razor (the principle of parsimony) to see whether they produce more comprehensive interpretations of the existing data.

THE ENGLISH SCHOOL

In this study the data are the play productions of children's minds. Numerous models of mental functioning exist, but few address themselves specifically to the play of children. One systematic, theoretical psychoanalytic model—the "English school" of Melanie Klein and her associates—was developed from the observation of young babies (including Klein's own children) and young children in school settings (Isaacs 1933). Very detailed records were kept of the children in spontaneous play at school, at home, and in the consulting room. Attempts were made to infer aspects of the children's development from studying these play protocols.

Klein, Fairbairn, Winnicott, and Balint stand out as theoreticians who have attempted model-building of the early emotional development of children in the paradigm that is now thought of as the object relations model. In order to facilitate conceptualization of the children's play, it is instructive to condense the Kleinian theoretical premises into a topographical model of emotional development.

25

One of Klein's objectives was to explain the interactions of the primitive emotional constellations, love (and its associated affects) and hate (and its associated affects) within the same character structure. Klein's model is developmentally phasic, with particular processes occurring as the baby matures physically and psychologically in a particular sequence. Her model has much in common with (one might even say it is a psychological extension of) the biogenetic law of Muller and Haeckel (that ontogeny recapitulates, in an abbreviated form, phylogeny). In this study I will examine parallels between the psychological development of the infant and the morphological processes that determine the growth and organization of the embryo.

Aristotle attempted to give a solution to the problem of ontogeny along the general lines of his philosophical teaching, distinguishing between the substance and the form of things (cited in Balinsky 1970). Aristotle supposed that the substance for a child's development is given by the mother, whereas the form (Aristotle used the phrase "creative principle") is supplied by the father. He thus accounted for the necessity of fertilization and asserted the stereotypes of men and women that persist today. Modern understanding of the storage and transmission of genetic information by the generative cells of both sexes has led to refinements of the contributions of mother and father to the child's development. Of particular value to this study are the linked ideas of (a) morphogenetic processes of increasing sophistication as the organism develops and (b) increasingly specific differentiation of function with maturation. It will become clear that the study of physical development can contribute to our ability to formulate models for the processes governing psychological development.

Since the mind is invisible, and yet many of our models are necessarily visual, it is conceptually useful to seek histological or topographical equivalents in our attempts to understand mental processes. Klein, noticing the perinatal differences in her children, thought of hereditary dispositions in the intensity and nature of affective experience. One child might feel hunger more intensely than another or might require more in the way of nurturing to be satisfied. Klein conceptualized the infant's first sensate experiences as (a) initially a need-free, thoroughly protected, and "comfortable" intrauterine period; (b) a painful (though possibly anesthetized) birth; and (c) exposure to the range of environmental stimuli and internal (biological) needs.

Because most babies depend for life on the breast or the bottle, Klein studied the baby's attachment to the breast by inferring intrapsychic processes from the baby's expressions at the breast. It would perhaps be helpful to adopt a written convention here. The "breast" denotes the baby's internally modified perception of the actual breast, and the breast (without the quotation marks) will be used to denote the physically real object. The "breast" is a complex perception that includes affective components and sensory distortions as well as the actual perception of the breast. Just as visual information is initially inverted and reduced on the retina, and subsequently processed in increasingly complex ways in the visual cortex, so the breast is internalized as the "breast" with many changes.

I think it would be fair to say that Klein's view of the "breast" was that it included such diverse factors as the mother's sense of well-being and her sense of emotional support from those around her. Klein saw that the breast could be an object of love and attachment and one of hate and rejection (as, for example, when it is needed but not available). The physically troubled child (e.g., babies with colic, a painful digestive condition) also may not experience the breast as purely pleasurable but may associate it with the imminent pain of the colic. Because of the extremes of emotion to which the young baby is prone, Klein postulates that a process of *splitting* occurs. In order to avoid the necessity of maintaining conflicting views of one and the same external object, she postulates that the breast is split into a "good breast" and a "bad breast," twin internalizations with opposite valences.

The child internalizes early experiences in relatively crude and simplistic ways. Internalization of an object depends on several factors: (a) the actual gratifying or depriving quality of the real object; (b) the child's associated affects to the object, which may be largely generated from internal preoccupations; and (c) the degree of significance of the object. Although it would be going too far to say that a new internal representation is formed each time the breast is presented to the baby, it is fair to say that the baby has several representations of the breast: a "good breast," a "bad breast," and various intermediate degrees of goodness and badness of "breast." Good internal objects are associated with the children's experiencing of their love feelings, bad objects with their hate feelings.

We can construct a simplified model of the personality using "good," "bad," and "neutral" objects in varying proportions and within some kind of organization or structure. This personality might (a) be balanced, (b) be dominated by bad objects, (c) be dominated by good objects, or (d) show widespread splitting.

In constructing the model, we need to consider the influence of the *content* or type of internalization on the developing personality and the *organization* of these contents—whether integrated, split, or partially integrated and partially split. The content-organization duality will be repeatedly observed in the models developed. These two factors are not independent. For most infants the nurturing-caretaking experiences are carefully planned and regulated (feeding, for example, takes place regularly to meet the infant's needs). Frightening or depriving experiences are not generally planned. Rather, they occur "by accident" or at random. Thus, the internalization of good objects occurs in a way that has intrinsic organization due to the extrinsic regularity of the nurturing experiences. We can speak of the coherent organization of the good object domain in the personality. Conversely, we might think of the bad object domain as rather poorly organized, with greater structural irregularity.

A natural feature of early parental care, the organization of benign experiences for the infant, thus leads to a later emotional tendency, namely, that of reacting adversely to unexpected situations. The fact that early, unpredictable situations have been frightening or depriving leads to this adverse reaction to later surprises. This example is, of course, quite limited and oversimplified, but it nevertheless illustrates a particular type of repetition compulsion, a characterological feature that leads to later organization of experience by the individual. This early experience might lead the child to arrange life so as to minimize change and to react adversely to inevitable change, such as the end of the school year or the change in routine of going on a vacation. I will now consider in a more systematic fashion the content and the organizational aspects of personality development.

CONTENT AND ARTICULATION
OF THE PERSONALITY

The Nature of Objects

An internal object is a mental structure that differs from an event in the real world in several important ways. Let us take the internal object, "the breast," as an example. The infant perceives the breast with touch, sight, smell, and taste, and adds to this multiple percept an emotional component that depends on the infant's internal state at the time (hungry, satisfied, sleepy, and so on). Also, "the breast" may be more or less familiar; a link with the memories of similar events will be made. The "breast" with these many components persists even when the breast itself is removed. Thus, whereas real world events happen and are gone, events in the internal object world endure.

The "breast" thus includes aspects of the breast itself, as well as the sound of the mother's voice, the feel of her body and of her arms cradling the baby, the sight of her face, the smell of her body, and the mood she brings to the baby. This last aspect of the mother is communicated to the baby through the other means mentioned. The breast has special significance because, apart from its life-sustaining function, the breast regularly enters and leaves the somatic boundary of the infant. When sealed inside the baby's lips, there is a continuity of the insides of the mother and baby. The nipple becomes, literally, an internal part of the baby. This process may be compared with the dissolution of body boundaries and of self-other distinction when the penis enters and is sealed inside the vagina during sexual intercourse.

Objects are described as "good" or "bad" depending on whether they are associated with nurturing, life-promoting, and comfort-bringing experiences or life-endangering and painful experiences, respectively. The "breast" may, for example, be a good object when a normally healthy baby is hungry, an indifferent object when the baby is satiated, or a bad object if the child is having a painful attack of colic.

In some circumstances, such as when there is an insufficiently graduated exposure to frustration that the child is unable to tolerate, the internal objects become overdetermined into "good" and "bad," with too few intermediate objects. This leads to a personality of extremes of mood in the child. The intermediate objects are often referred to as "neutralizing" objects in view of their role in balancing these extremes. The phenomenon of polarization of objects into good and bad (splitting) reduces the child's ability later in life to distinguish realistic threats and realistically nurturing situations.

The Organization of Objects

Various experiences present themselves to the child in more or less regular ways. Feeding tends to be arranged so that it occurs regularly and is thus available to prediction and habit. Such regular experiences (feeding, sleeping, being kept warm and dry) are internalized in an orderly fashion. The regularity of these domains of internalization is maintained by a class of objects known as structuring internalizations. These give form and regularity to the character and provide the basis for the concept of "character structure." The recently popular idea of "borderline personality organization" refers to individuals in whom there are areas of coherent structuring introjects, producing an interestingly mixed diagnostic picture.

As mentioned earlier, the domains in the personality dominated by the good objects tend to be more regularly organized than the domains dominated by the bad objects, and that is because threatening or persecutory experiences are not generally arranged for the child in the way that caring experiences are. This leads to the tendency, in later life, for surprises or any unexpected event to arouse alarm and fright due to the activation of this less well organized aspect of the personality; whereas planning, which requires the use of prediction and expectation, can usually be accomplished in an air of optimism and hope.

The Libidinal Investment of an Object

The degree of interest a child invests in a particular experience depends on the significance of that experience. Thus, internal objects may be highlighted with more or less libidinal energy. "Breast" and "feces" may be strongly cathected, whereas "ceiling" and "doorknob" may be relatively uncathected. The degree of libidinal investment is not constant, and it comes to be partly under ego and superego control. Distorted vicissitudes of libidinal cathexis are seen most clearly in fetishes and some other perversions.

Boundary Phenomena

The limits of the personality are neither clearly definable nor simple. In fact, there is a complex range of boundary phenomena that become elaborated in the child from birth and that become more crystallized over the years from adolescence. Certain generalizations are nevertheless possible. At birth, the physical continuity of existence maintained in the womb is translated into a fusion of identity in which the personality boundaries of mother and baby are continuous within one another. It may be more accurate to say that the baby's unformed personality is assumed within the personality boundaries of the mother.

This fusion is associated with a symbiotic interdependency. Neither mother nor baby can perceive accurately the boundary between them, the mother confusing primitive affects coming from the baby with those coming from her own self. The baby experiences even interoceptive phenomena as if they come "from outside" because there is no clear internal-external discrimination. In particular, babies feel their own anger as external, as if it were a threat from outside. Persisting into later life, this would be seen as paranoid projection, and one would think of "delusions of persecution." This early phase is known as the "paranoid position." Persistence of the phase of symbiotic attachment into later childhood appears as an exaggerated, mutual maternal-child preoccupation. Klein saw the emergence from the paranoid position as the onset of a crucial developmental step toward mature relatedness to others, the depressive position. This position will be discussed below.

Transitional Objects

Freud (1920) described the child's use of the "throwaway" game as the point of beginning sensitivity to the comings and goings of the mother. The baby throws away a cup or spoon repeatedly, as often as it is recovered by an obliging grown-up. The spoon thus goes between the adult and the baby, and between the baby and himself or herself.

Pacifiers, cuddly toys, or "security" blankets are also used by the baby to "stand in" between the baby and the mother in the mother's absence. The investment in the mother as a comforting presence is partly replicated by the investment in a cuddly toy, a blanket, or a pacifier. This object stands between the mother in her presence and the mother in her absence, in terms of its libidinal significance and symbolic value. It comes to stand between the child and the outside world when the child begins playing throwaway games.

The infant is thus, in effect, developing a strategy for the maintenance of personality equilibrium in the face of loss or separation. In general, we could infer that the child is finding ways to link possibly disturbing experiences (e.g., loss, maternal absence) with the opposite experience of comfort and reassurance (the maternal presence). In internal object terms the child is formulating a link between good and bad object domains of inner experience.

Within the character structure, it therefore follows that the internalized transitional objects act to stand between the more stable good and bad objects and are thus bridging or neutralizing objects. The "transitional object" (i.e., the internal object) can be a representation of the real world, or it can be an image, a symbol, or an idea with only partial derivative connections to external reality. In adult mentation, ideas used as transitional objects act to buffer the self from the turbulent possibilities of emotional reactions to day-to-day events; they are thus part of the self's defensive operations.

In this study I will examine the child's use of imagination, of fantasy production, in the recovery from developmental trauma. I will advance the hypothesis that transitional object phenomena are used in both the repair and the maintenance of healthy personality operations, that transitional objects are important in normal development and are particularly important in a child's therapeutic recovery. Evidence in support or contradiction of this hypothesis will be adduced from the detailed examination of the themes in the child's play. The links between play and other manifestations of the child's fantasy life, particularly dreams and their function, will be analyzed.

The various object types described above and their articulation within the personality structure are topographically illustrated in Figures 1-7.

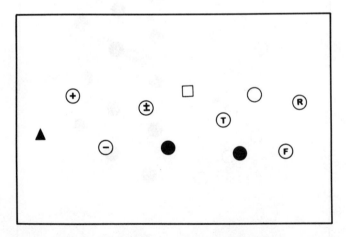

Figure 1. The variety of objects: a symbolic representation showing that objects may have a range of varying qualities (good, bad, intermediate) or may be structuring, transitional, rigid or flexible, amplifying or neutralizing, transmuting or "sinks" (which absorb and surround existing objects).

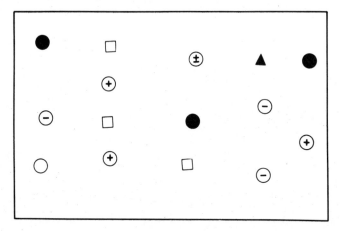

Figure 2. A field of various objects, these objects well intermixed and coherently arranged.

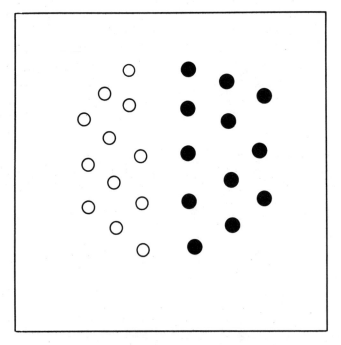

Figure 3. "Splitting" in operation: objects are arbitrarily divided into only two types, good and bad, each with its own domain in the personality.

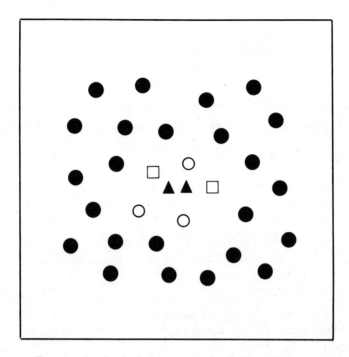

Figure 4. Domination by bad objects: a personality with a small healthy core surrounded by (dominated by) "bad objects" (shown as solid black circles).

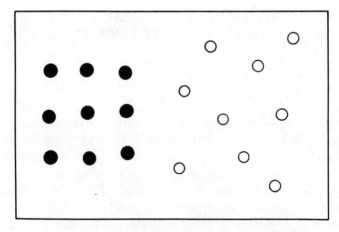

Figure 5. Differential organization of good and bad objects: a personality in which the "good objects" (black circles) are rigidly organized, whereas the "bad objects" are more loosely organized.

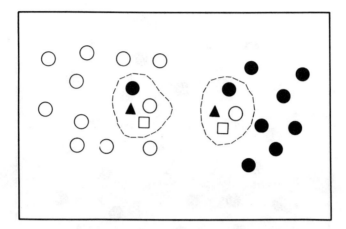

Figure 6. Two individuals, one of whom is dominated by bad objects, the other dominated by good objects. Relationship is nevertheless possible through the sharing of objects common to both (inside dotted lines), leading perhaps to some exchange of dissimilar objects and to the diversification of both personalities.

INDIVIDUATION AND THE ONSET OF THE DEPRESSIVE POSITION

As the baby advances in the internalization of complex object systems, a developmental process supervenes that changes the quality of the child's experience. The change is partly associated with an emotional and often literal weaning of the child, preparatory to a more mature independence and to physical locomotion (crawling and walking). More important, however, the change heralds the beginning of an independent *identity* for the child, one in which the child's own reactions are differentiated from the reactions of others. In other words, it is at this stage that the co-experience of unconscious phenomena in the mother and the child begins to break down. Baby and mother begin to differentiate their individual reactions, and the process known as individuation begins to occur.

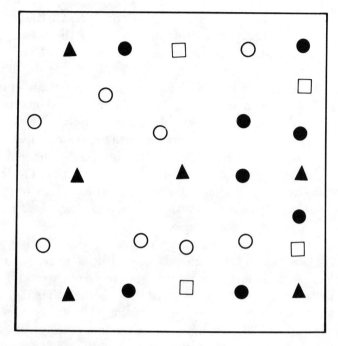

Figure 7. A part of a balanced personality: a small part of a complex personality with some aspects of flexibility, some of rigidity—a varied repertoire of objects and systems.

As mentioned earlier, much of Klein's thinking is given over to the origins of the experiences of love and hate and to the complex problem of their interdigitation in an internal state of emotional equilibrium within the personality. During this phase of development, a new problem arises for the child in the experience of his or her newly owned anger toward the now external breast. The threat is that of destroying or losing (driving away) the still nurturing breast through one's anger (actually, dyscathectic rage) toward it. Note that the possibility now exists for the breast to be held as an ambivalently regarded object, providing splitting has not occurred too drastically.

One way the child temporarily removes the threat to the external breast (and to himself or herself in the loss of the breast) is to attack the self with retroflected rage. This process is the precursor, mutatis mutandis, of the child's capacity to experience guilt, remorse, and self-recrimination, and the consequent wish to make amends. It is in this making of amends, the fantasized or symbolic reconstruction of the damaged object, that a new, more mature style of relatedness with the mother as a separate individual is forged. The successful resolution of the depressive position thus involves the development of the capacity for *reparation*. The theme of early separation from and later reunion with parents or parent figures is embodied in many myths and legends (e.g., the Princess and the Pea, and the Moses legend).

The classical Kleinian idea of reparation includes a fairly weakly defined disposition to make amends or restitution to aspects of the other that one feels one's own aggression has damaged. This urge is felt to be enhanced by identification with the other (the good object: the "breast"). By an extension of these ideas, the concept of reparation can be elaborated. The individuation of the infant from the psychological matrix of the mother-world-child continuum occurs gradually and is incomplete when the depressive position begins. Indeed it is the ability to dyscathect the other that permits individuation to occur.

Therefore, a first extension of Klein's ideas on reparation is that the process includes not only restitution to the other, whom one has in fantasy damaged by one's aggression, but it also includes restorative actions to the aspects of oneself felt to have been damaged by one's own (projected) hate, greed, and aggression.

The depressive position also allows for "whole object" relations; that is, instead of the breast being seen as two (or many) part objects (good, bad, and so on), the breast is seen ambivalently as a single whole object. Reparation can thus be seen as involving the synthesis or linking of formerly split objects or, by extension, of formerly split object domains within the personality. In the topographical model described, the splits are brought together by the use of bridging or transitional introjects. Just as the cuddly toy "stands between" the mother in her presence and the mother in her absence, other internalized representations of the world, or autochthonous ideas about the world, stand between a traumatized aspect of the self and a well-endowed aspect of the personality.

Taking these two extensions of Kleinian theory together, we can hypothesize as follows: In effective mentation not only are reparative themes devised to make restitution to "the world" for damage inflicted on it but also specific transitional themes; the latter serve to link traumatized or deprived aspects of the self, which have been split off, encapsulated, or otherwise "fixated," to more benign or nurtured aspects of the self. That is to say, in the depressive position, the self goes from a collection of split-off, "part" objects to a complex, unified, and more coherent system of linked, whole objects.

In examining the themes of play, as they reflect the child's spontaneous imagery, we can seek the particular themes that reflect aspects of the character structure (see Chapter 6 for a clinical discussion). It is also possible to discover central foci of distress or dominant conflicts in the child's development by a study of the child's own play productions. The ways in which the child devises reparative themes to address these central "core" conflicts will reveal something of the nature of the reparative processes naturally available to the child. The analogy with the somatic immune system's techniques for developing antigen-specific antibodies lends itself to the illustration of this equivalent psychological process.

Before considering the data from the study, it is helpful to examine in more detail the genesis of Klein's own ideas of the extent and variety of the processes of reparation.

3
The Concept of Reparation

KLEIN'S EARLIEST IDEAS

It is instructive to trace the evolution of Klein's thinking toward the idea of reparation and to see to what extent she herself was able to elaborate and redefine her original concept.

In her earliest published work Klein (1921) had concluded that whereas in normal children unconscious fantasies are expressed in play activities, the simultaneous inhibition of play and of unconscious fantasy would act as a developmental block in the neurotic child. She saw this inhibition as caused by the unacceptably frightening nature of the child's fantasy life, which was thus lost from access or expression. These terrifying fantasies tended to be of a sexual or aggressive nature.

An important part of her treatment technique, therefore, was enabling the child to face some of these primitive fantasies through the support and encouragement of the analyst. She did not, as is commonly supposed, depend in large degree on her interpretations as a health-promoting agent. Indeed, in one early case she states that she "only quite occasionally and more as a hint rendered this or that matter conscious" (Klein 1921, p. 39). Klein adds, "Moreover, I got the impression from the whole trend of his [Fritz's] phantasies and games, and from occasional remarks, that part of his complexes had become conscious for himself and I considered that this sufficed" (p. 39). Of another child, she remarked, "I had a great wealth of material that remained uninterpreted" (p. 42).

In her first days, therefore, one can see that Klein was tentatively exploring the nature and meaning of the child's fantasy life and was quite consciously refraining from much interpretation. She may have had the idea of a latent, spontaneously curative aspect of the child's mind that was capable of liberation through play.

43

By 1923 Klein had refined her thinking sufficiently to present her ideas on the psychoanalysis of children, including the symptoms that could be expected in the neurotically inhibited child. These symptoms included little or no pleasure in learning, awkwardness in or distaste for play, so-called "laziness," and others. She pointed out that these and other inhibitions are related to anxiety. The dissolution of the inhibitions in play therapy gives rise to a progressively increasing anxiety, which gradually subsides after it has reached a certain point. She stressed that the therapeutic aim was not merely the removal of inhibitions but the restoration of the "primary pleasure of the activity" (Klein 1923, p. 78).

Here Klein also expanded her idea of the play function. She pointed out that in their play children symbolically represent fantasies, wishes, and experiences. They employ in play the same phylogenetically acquired mode of representation seen in dreams. Play could thus be said to be the "golden road" to the child's unconscious.

Besides this archaic mode of representation, children employ another means of representation: they substitute actions (the original precursors of thought) for words. With children, acting becomes a prominent part. (Wax [1973] has pointed out that the inability to pretend, the failure of this means of expression, can be a major contributor to the pathology of the borderline child.) Klein (1926, pp. 135-136) gives this example: Ruth as an infant had gone hungry for some time because her mother had little milk to give her. At the age of 4 years and 3 months, when playing in the water basin, she called the water tap the "milk tap." She declared that the milk was running into mouths (the holes in the drain) but that very little was flowing. This unsatisfied desire made its appearance in countless games and dramatizations and in her whole attitude. For instance, she asserted that she was "poor," that she had only one coat, that she had very little to eat—although none of these statements accorded with external reality.

Klein's observations of these children are echoed in and expanded by the cases presented in this study.

THE BEGINNING OF
CHILD ANALYSIS IN LONDON

In both of these cases Klein was supervised by Abraham until his death in 1925. Klein came to London at Ernest Jones's invitation and was to settle there. In London she presented her ideas to the British Psychoanalytic Society and was met with vociferous opposition that led her to clarify the theoretical basis of her technique.

For example, she responded to the publication of Anna Freud's "Introduction to the Technique of the Analysis of Children" (1927) with a symposium paper. Anna Freud then felt that children were not ready to enter into a transference neurosis, a new edition of their love relations, because their original love objects—the parents —still existed as objects in reality. Anna Freud thought that one of the tasks in treating the child was to reinforce a weakly formed superego, whereas Klein thought the task was to diminish an archaic, punitive superego. Anna Freud's patient, a child of 4, had described in play her fight with and eventual victory over her devil. The child told Freud that she had helped her "not to be so unhappy at having to be stronger than it" (p. 49). This illustrates the reinforcement of the child's healthy superego. Klein felt that the child's early fixations had not been adequately addressed.

These theoretical disputes were in part the growing pains of child analysis, with its vast areas of ignorance and areas on the brink of discovery. By 1929 Klein had begun to formulate the ideas of splitting and the ways in which early splitting mechanisms are reflected in the child's affective style. These mechanisms are more fully described in Chapter 2. Of relevance of Klein's formulation of reparation was the crucial observation that the child's play contained representations with fantastically bad and fantastically good characteristics. These represent, respectively, intermediate stages between the terrible, menacing (even persecutory) superego, which is wholly divorced from reality, and the identifications that approximate reality more closely (i.e., the good objects, the internalizations of the caring breast).

Of special importance is Klein's reference to these archaic and polarized images as being "intermediate figures." She felt that these intermediates (i.e., these intermediate play representations) evolved into more neutral figures, closer to the reality of the normal vicissitudes of parental care, and that this evolution could regularly be observed in the course of play therapy. For example, a child may begin by showing, in the drama of play, scenes in which helpless individuals lose battle after battle with huge and daunting monsters. Gradually, the individuals become less helpless, and the monsters evolve into, perhaps, circus animals—trainable and yet fierce. Note that Klein felt these monstrous presentations were themselves feeble (intermediate) representations of the true fears and fantasms in the child's mind. She also described these fantasms as being projected in an indiscriminate way onto the parents, other adults, playmates, and so forth.

Thus, she described a result of play therapy that is confirmed in this study: because of the dissolution of the effect of these primitive fantasies that are dominating the child, the emotional relation of the child to the parents improves. Other suggestions will be offered as to the genesis of the early improvement in the parental relation in the analysis of the data of this study.

Klein (1929a) gave an illustration of the child's domination by "dangerous" fantasies in the case of George:

> George, who at the time was six years old, brought me for months on end a series of phantasies in which he, as the mighty leader of a band of savage huntsmen and wild animals, fought, conquered and cruelly put to death his enemies who also had wild beasts to support them. The animals were then eaten. The battle never came to an end as new enemies always appeared. (p. 201)

In reality George had consciously thought that he was surrounded and threatened by magicians, witches, and soldiers. The allies invented by George in his play are mirrored in those of a 4½-year-old boy who invented a magic fairy who healed with her wand all the wounds inflicted by the play enemies. In a footnote, Klein (1929a) notes:

The further the play analysis continues, the less powerful does the influence of the threatening figures become and the more strongly and lastingly do the wish fulfilling figures appear; at the same time there is a proportionate increase in the desire to play, and in the satisfaction at the end of the games. Pessimism has diminished; optimism has increased. (p. 205)

FIRST IDEAS ABOUT REPARATION

In the first 10 years of her work with children Klein had observed some of the mutative processes at work in play therapy and had formulated some of the developmental mechanisms, such as splitting, contributing to the child's distress. Significantly, it was in the writing of a paper in which she discussed no clinical material at all that her first ideas about reparation came to her mind. In 1929 Klein examined an opera by Ravel, *The Magic Word*, and a literary work, *The Empty Space*, by Karen Michaelis (cited in Klein 1929b).

In the opera a child flies into a rage, frustrated by his mother's threat to give him "dry bread and no sugar in your tea" for supper as a punishment for not doing his homework. He smashes the room to bits—the grandfather clock, the chair, the sofa. But the things he has broken come to life and attack him. "Away with the dirty little creature," the table cries.

The child staggers out of the house and seeks refuge in the park. The animals there fight over who shall be first to bite him, and a squirrel who has been bitten in the debate falls screaming to the ground. *The boy instinctively takes his scarf and binds up the little creature's paw.* This act of generosity in the midst of his terror amazes the animals, and they sing (in a chorus), "That's a very good child." The child's self-redemption, by helping the squirrel, is seen by Klein as a manifestation of a fundamental developmental motif: the desire to make reparation, to make good for injuries done to the world or to its psychological antecedent, the breast.

The work by Michaelis is a biographical story about the development of the painting ability in Michaelis's friend, Ruth Kjar. Kjar was subject to fits of suicidal depression, which she described by saying, "There is an empty space in me, which I can never fill" (Klein 1929b, p. 215). When she married, she was perfectly happy for a short while; then the despair returned. Kjar had decorated her house artistically to the point that it was almost "a gallery of modern art." But before Christmas her brother-in-law had taken back a picture he had loaned her, leaving an empty space on one wall. "The empty space grinned hideously down on her" (p. 215). Her husband suggested she try to paint a picture herself; the picture she produced was a masterpiece of painting. After this, to her own amazement, Kjar went on to produce several masterly works and had them exhibited to critics and to the public.

Again, Klein sees the restoration of the self through the filling of the "empty space" as a reparative move that overcomes internal fantasies of having destroyed another person vital to oneself (or a part of oneself) through one's own aggression. A link is also made between reparation and sublimation. In these examples reparation is a special form of sublimation. In this paper Klein makes first mention of the idea of reparation and anticipates her later work by pointing out that "in development, the fear of an attacking mother gives way to the fear of losing a real loving mother" (p. 217). She thus describes what is later to be seen as the transition between the paranoid and the depressive phases.

It was some years later that Klein returned to the theme of reparation, again not as part of a clinical paper but as an unprepared oral presentation (1934) at a symposium on crime. In this instance also, Klein's ideas were not part of a carefully reasoned clinical exposition. Rather, they were made at very short notice (a couple of days) in a presentation to a symposium on the "rampant" problem of crime in the streets of London. Klein (1927) had already considered the origins of antisocial tendencies in normal children. She felt that the combination of criminal tendencies, both in the commission of the act and in the compulsion to seek punishment, represented the child's attempt at mastery of a situation in which, in fantasy, cruel retaliation was expected for "bad thoughts," such as aggressive fantasies directed toward the parents. Klein thought that almost any punishment inflicted by normal parents would be very reassuring to the child faced with his or her own fantasies of murderous attacks by the parents. This theme has recently been taken up again by Dorothy Bloch (1976), who examines children's fantasies of being murdered by their parents for any little "badness" or mischief.

In this short (five-minute) presentation Klein (1934) did not consider the instances of hardened criminal adults whose parents had indeed acted as if to fulfill the imagined, cruel persecution of the child. She did point out, however, that in normally developing children, aggressive or sadistic instincts (shown in tearing, cutting, breaking, burning kinds of play) alternate with severe anxiety and eventually with guilt. She sees the restitutive process as a corollary and complement to the sadism and aggression of the young child. Reparation is seen as a later mirror image of early paranoid anxiety. Rather than being cowed by a persecutory world, the child senses the urge to make reparative gestures toward the damaged world. In other words, as this (persecutory) anxiety diminishes in the normal course of development or in the play analysis of a fixated child, feelings of guilt and constructive tendencies come to the fore. Whereas the child had done nothing but chop bits of wood to pieces, later he tried to *assemble* them.

Klein mentions the accelerating iatrogenic cycle: the more the tendency to restitute grows, the milder the superego becomes, and vice versa. That is, the balance of libido in the personality structure shifts in such a way as to render the course, the direction, of development benign rather than pathogenic. This crucial developmental feature will be seen to recur as a model of therapeutic change in this study.

REPARATION AS A
FORERUNNER OF AUTONOMY

In 1935 Klein's ideas of restitutive tendencies were becoming more sharply defined in the developmental line of the child. The early, fearful view of the world held by the child, wherein the child's own aggression was felt to be coming from "outside" (by the mechanism of paranoid projection), gives way to a view of the world as partly benign and partly depriving, and it is this world toward which the child's aggression is directed. At 6 months, the child becomes physically more motile and curiosity expands. Teething and weaning both contribute to the child's developing autonomy. In the transition between the paranoid position (in which aggression is felt to impinge on the self from without) and the depressive position (in which aggression is felt to be a dangerous force inside the child), the preservation of external good objects (e.g., the feeding breast) is felt to be synonymous with the preservation of the ego. The symbiotically possessed breast gives way to an extrinsic object that is in danger of being damaged or driven away by the anger felt toward it in its more depriving moments.

In order to make restitution for the imagined damage caused by aggressive fantasies, the ego embarks on a reparative (Klein uses the word "restorative") course. This may also be seen as pre-emptively trying to prevent the breast from being driven away by the child's dyscathectic aggression. The process is far more than a mere reaction formation against the aggressive fantasies. The ego is impelled by its identification with the good object (the breast) to make this restitution, to preserve the self through repair of the other. It is not altogether clear whether Klein limits this concept to the repair of damage thought to have already been caused by aggressive thoughts and fantasies, or whether the restorative move arises simultaneously with the awareness of the breast as an external object, subject to attack by the child's aggressive fantasies.

This paper (Klein 1935) prepared the way for a turning point in Kleinian theory and what can be seen as the pivotal point in the development of Klein's ideas. These ideas have not been substantially changed, nor more clearly stated since Klein and Riviere (1937) presented them in a series of talks on "The Emotional Life of Civilised Men and Women" at Caxton Hall in London in 1936. Their papers contain the central ideas of Klein's metapsychology of development: for Klein maturation consists of the attempts to integrate the conflicting aspects of two constellations of emotions —the love and the hate constellations. These ideas have been carried forward in contemporary thought with little modification.

SPLITTING AND REPARATION

Object relations theory seeks to explain mental processes in terms of the intermodulation of love and hate (or libido and Thanatos) within the personality. The model includes ideas about the content of fantasy life (the nature of objects) and about organizing aspects of the personality (structural introjects) that serve to regulate the interrelationship of the parts and influences in the character structure. The splitting of various parts of the personality from one another is seen as a major determinant of the characteristics of the individual. The nature and degree of the splitting, together with the degree to which the splits are bridged within the personality, determine the adaptive capacity of the overall structure.

Klein developed the concept of reparation to describe the ego's efforts to restore damaged aspects of the self and of the mother, who is perceived to have been damaged by the infant's primitive aggression.

CONSTITUTIONALLY DETERMINED EMOTIONAL DISPOSITIONS

Klein, reflecting on the dramatic differences in infants' emotional reactivity even from the moment of birth, suggested a preexisting set of tendencies or dispositions that would color the infant's perceptions and emotional reactions to the range of environmental stimuli. (Klein herself had borne three children, and her theory is in part based on her observations as a mother.) Some children, she suggested, might perhaps feel "hungry," however much they were fed. Others might be more needy of nurturance in order to feel satisfied. Therefore, although some weight is given to the nature of mothering, there is also consideration of the idiosyncratic perceptions of that mothering that one child, and not another, might have.

In particular Klein felt that the neonatal period itself created prototypes that would become the basis of a very early type of transference reaction. This reaction, in turn, would change the child's perception of all subsequent experiences. For example, it is observed that babies who do not or cannot form an attachment in the first days after birth show an exaggerated neediness in the months that follow. If the lack of attachment is sustained too long, the child shows an irreversible lack of receptivity to care, and death may ensue (Bowlby 1951). Klein would say of the first instance that the initial period of unmet need produced a state of "domination by bad objects," which was shown by an exaggerated petulance, demandingness, and rage. Only greatly intensified maternal care could redress the internal balance.

THE BALANCE OF THE PERSONALITY

The spontaneous function of play in the life of the child includes cathartic, symbolic, representational, and integrative aspects (Isaacs 1933, Sechehaye 1950, Lowenfeld 1950, Winnicott 1971b, respectively). The maintenance of the equilibrium of the personality occurs through the combination of these play functions with the reality relationships of the child.

Object relations postulates a developmental line in which there are internal determinants, each of which requires a particular degree of maternal care and of maternal frustration of the child. A simple example is the baby's unmet need for graduated exposure to life's challenges. Uncontrolled events (such as medical complications of birth, illness, or accidents) may offer a wide range of challenges to the child's developing personality. Maternal absence is known to be accommodated by older babies (over 2 months) through the use of transitional objects, such as a cuddly toy or security blanket. These serve as objects that lie in between the present mother and the absent mother in their significance to the child.

TRANSITIONAL REGULATING MECHANISMS

The function of the transitional object is complex in its range of operation. Transitional objects can be mental events, with no direct external correlates, as well as material objects, such as a cuddly toy. Consideration will be given in the present work to the ways in which transitional objects serve in the regulation of the internal balance of the personality, both in normal development and when the child is challenged beyond the internal limits of frustration tolerance.

Lesser challenges appear to activate reparative mechanisms in the healthy child that act like antibodies to neutralize dangerous, invading traumata. These reparative mechanisms are discussed in detail in the theoretical exposition of Kleinian theory in Chapter 2. It will suffice to say here that the variety, strength, and repertoire of the transitional-object system determine the adaptability of the personality to a less than perfect environment.

Winnicott has come to speak of "good enough mothering" to describe the level of care the child finds acceptable (that is, care which is within the limits of the child's ability to compensate for the day-to-day conflicts to which she or he is exposed). The model thus includes not only ideas of "adequate care" but also of spontaneous reparative mechanisms within the personality of the healthy child.

THE ESTABLISHMENT OF
INTERNAL CONFLICTS

If there is a disturbance in the child's development that antedates the establishment of adequate reparative mechanisms, or overwhelms the established mechanisms, then a problematic nexus of internal conflict occurs. The child may become, for example, fearful and timid. Extra parental efforts may relieve the problem or mask its expression, or they may be quite ineffective. In the latter case the child and parents embark on a career of domination by a developmental fixation.

For example, a child who had suffered a painful burn in an accident at the stove at the age of 20 months changed from his previously benign self to a child driven between extremes of quietness and great petulance, defiance, and rage. The mother was able to tolerate this by being more patient, concerned, and devoted to this child (at some cost to her other children), and it was not until the child began school that treatment was sought.

In another example, a child whose suckling experience had been traumatized by severe and almost continuous colic (a form of epigastric distress of unknown origin) became cut off and withdrawn from all loving approaches by either parent. Nothing they could do seemed to penetrate her isolation. Again, after some years of failure despite their concerted efforts, therapeutic help was sought.

THE PLAY THERAPY PARADIGM

The play therapy model regards the spontaneous reparative mechanisms as having been inhibited or overwhelmed by some developmental trauma or pattern of traumata. The therapeutic influence consists of allowing the child to readdress the trauma through a regressive recapitulation of the trauma in play.

This study addresses the question of evidence, from the records of children in play therapy, for the hypothesis of an emergent reparative mechanism. Second, the study examines the way in which the reparative mechanism is tailored to suit the particular child's developmental, intrapsychic problem.

The study is partly theoretical, examining the development of the ideas of reparation, and it is partly clinical, examining certain limited and specific epiphenomena of the treatment situation at a particular point in the child's treatment.

4
The Clinical Approach

The method of the study is a retrospective examination of the records of some 30 children seen in an outpatient child psychotherapy practice over a period of two years. Among the criteria for this larger group are (a) definitive therapeutic changes shown by the children, as judged by their parents' and teachers' reports; (b) a circumscribed period of treatment following a prolonged illness (a protracted and sustained period of disability or distress) with marked symptoms. This clear morbidity, manifest in a range of symptoms and in the general emotional disposition of the child, is designed to avoid spurious "improvements" from nonexistent illnesses, which would not illustrate therapeutic effects.

All the children are prelatency in order to avoid the masking effect of the repression mechanisms and defense mechanisms of the latency period on the child's fantasy life.

EXEMPLARY PROTOCOLS

The records of these 30 children were examined to find two protocols that most clearly serve the purposes of this research. Although one case would be sufficient to illustrate the nature of the reparative motif, two will be chosen so that the emergence of the motif in two different play modalities (verbal and nonverbal) may be illustrated. Additional requirements for the choice of the two were the availability of adequately detailed developmental histories to permit inference of early influences on the child, and a sufficiently rich form of expressive play therapy to allow analysis of the themes present in the child's play.

57

It should be emphasized that these protocols were selected precisely to illustrate the hypothetical motif most clearly. The study does not try to show that all children who recover in the course of expressive play therapy do so through the generation of the reparative motif, although this offers a promising avenue for more extensive study of the prevalence of the reparative motif.

The validity of the concept of the reparative motif as a reflection of character change will be assessed both from theoretical propositions and from the detailed examination of the course of recovery of the selected cases. The generalizability of the conclusions drawn from the selected cases will be addressed by reference to the nonselected cases in the larger group. These nonselected cases also will be used to illustrate other interesting aspects of the reparative motif, such as the role of the reparative motif as an intermediary between the child and the therapist, or between the child's own personality strengths and conflicts.

The data for the study consist of historical records, photographs of Worlds, and transcriptions of children's stories as they were told. These records are voluminous, and some selection for relevance will be made. Examples of play showing a "damaged" motif will be provided so that the reader may readily see the changing nature of the play during the course of therapy. Analysis of many hundreds of photographs of Worlds by the practiced eye of the experienced clinician reveals certain patterns that will be self-evident to less trained eyes that know what to look for. Although the symbolism of play is open to a variety of interpretations, care will be taken to justify any assumptions made through reference to a coherent body of knowledge.

The analysis of the data consists of making links between the observed themes in play and the theoretical predictions derived partly from the extension of Kleinian thoughts on reparation and partly from the history of each child's development. The extent to which the theoretical predictions are supported and contradicted by the play motif will be used to develop further understanding of the process of reparation. This will have implications for other clinicians, who will be able to use the techniques developed in this study in the analysis of their own work, and for the field of child development in general. In the latter case, it may be possible to use the knowledge gained in this work to divine the presence and operation of reparative mechanisms through the observation of normal children in the course of their daily play.

Illustrations of the data showing contrasting examples of pathognomonic and reparative motifs follow. One is taken from the World technique, the other from stories told by children about their imaginative play.

EXAMPLES OF CHILDREN'S EXPRESSIVE PLAY IN PLAY THERAPY

Each of the following examples illustrates the kind of scene a child might produce in play therapy. The reader should apply the following criteria to each scene in turn, to allow inference to be made about the quality and level of the child's experience of his or her inner world.

What is the apparent content of the scene/story? For example, it might involve (a) conflict, (b) pain, (c) death/destruction, (d) impoverishment, (e) constriction, (f) unmet vital needs (such as hunger, cold, lack of shelter, abandonment). Or the tone might be (a) benign, (b) hopeful, (c) protected, (d) satisfied, (f) rich, diverse, varied.

What is the level of organizational coherence? This may range from compulsive to chaotic, or there may be mixed levels of organization in different parts of the scene.

What, if any, is the direction the theme and organization are taking? Is the theme descending into more morbid, terrifying ideation or becoming more disorganized? Or is it becoming more coherent, harmonious, benign, and hopeful?

Matthew

The examples from Matthew's case show sand play scenes and brief descriptions of the scenes by the child. The scenes were produced some months apart.

Example 1. The scene shown in Figure 8 was produced by a child (born of a mentally retarded mother) who was looked after and is reported to have been sexually and physically abused by his maternal grandparents. The scene was produced at the beginning of treatment.

The child's description was "There was an accident. People are screaming, yelling for help. The police cars and ambulances try to come. They all crash. Everybody dies."

In this scene the major themes are pain, lack of control, the unavailability of help, and eventual death. Note also the weak organization of the scene.

Example 2. The same child produced the scene shown in Figure 9 when treatment was well underway. The child's descrip-

Figure 8. An accident.

One planet
"The spaceships crashed."

Another planet
"They have more rescue vehicles."

Huge fire   Tiny fire truck   Connecting ladder and hoses   Large fire truck and ambulances

Figure 9. An articulated rescue scene.

61

tion was "Two spaceships crashed. There was a huge fire. The trucks came to help, but they could not put out the fire. The firemen built a ladder to where there was more water and ambulances. They put out the fire. People were hurt and taken to the hospital."

Again in this scene we see evidence of trauma, but there is a new relationship to the potential sources of rescue: although they are far away, a bridge is built to enable them to be used. The bridge is thus a transitional object used to recruit help from one part of the perceived scene to add to an endangered part. Note also the improved organization of this scene.

Example 3. Matthew produced the scene shown in Figure 10 toward the end of his treatment. Note the progression from destruction to organization since the previous scenes: "This is a town. The cars here are stopped to let the others go by. Over here is the school and the firehouse. The people just live in the town. They are going shopping. The bus is going to New York. The truck is bringing more gas to the gas station."

In this scene we see a supervening organization within which the other activities occur. There is a regulation of the traffic, both by the existence of streets and by the child's handmade traffic

Figure 10. David's town.

signs. Movement still occurs, but it appears to be in constructive directions. There are references to what might be thought of as the child's current reality (e.g., school).

In the transformation apparent in these scenes we can translate the play themes into object relations terms. The first scene can be regarded as a manifestation of both conflicted and disorganized object relations, with weak internal structures and poor regulation of impulses (particularly aggression, although the construction of the "accidents" may be seen to have some sexual qualities if examined in detail). The earliest scenes proceeded in their depravity to a "crash of the century" (Figure 11); and then the theme shifted to the second scene shown, wherein a new theme emerges: the reparative theme, in which the balance shifts to a more hopeful direction. The third scene shows the postreparative neutrality, with little in the way of frightening or exaggerated affects.

Kevin

The examples from Kevin's case consist of stories he told during therapy over a period of several weeks.

Example 1.

One day this boy was walking down the street near his home—it's College Avenue—when suddenly he is pushed into a black sedan. The next thing he knows is he is being driven at 90 miles an hour toward the Eastshore Freeway with the police chasing them.

One of the crooks notices the boy is awake so they hit him on the head with a baseball bat. Crash. Crack. Cream. "Ouch," said the boy. We don't know what happens next.

This child had in reality been adopted and was painfully afraid of being "sent away" again. Note the cruel aggression in the theme, the sense of being stolen, and the loss of control over himself.

Figure 11. Crash of the century.

Example 2.

There was once a little fire engine who was not a very big fire engine. There had never been an emergency when he had had to help. One day there was such a big fire that two whole firehouses had to help.

The buildings were burning up. All the fire engines got out their hoses. All the people had got out in time, but there was another person who hadn't gotten out. One fire engine spotted the person. That was the little fire engine.

The little fire engine got out its ladder and one of the firemen yelled to the person to climb down the ladder. The chief fireman said to the people who watched the fire, "Give three cheers for the little fire engine. Hip, Hip, Hooray! Hip, Hip, Hooray! Hip, Hip, HOORAY!" And the little fire engine became a hero.

In this scene the lack of recognition reflected the child's narcissistic impoverishment, and indeed he was nosologically a narcissistic child. Note that in the theme the insignificant fire engine becomes a hero and is recognized for his importance in spite of his small size. Also note in this scene the recurrence of the ladder theme, also used by Matthew. The ladder, as a tool, enables one to climb to perilously inaccessible places. Symbolically, the ladder represents these children's reaching into previously inaccessible parts of themselves for strength.

5
The Setting

The practice of expressive play therapy, even within the psychoanalytic tradition, is somewhat heterogeneous and is not well described in the literature. The model used in this study is fairly typical of European child guidance clinics, although there are certainly idiosyncrasies brought in through my own inclinations and through the necessities of practice in the United States. In order to clarify some of the features of the setting in which the data were obtained, I will briefly describe the ways in which a child enters treatment. This is not a description of the techniques of expressive play therapy per se but rather a description of the context in which play therapy takes place in my own practice.

THE COMMUNITY

I am known locally for my interest in the treatment of young children in the 3- to 8-year age range, although I do sometimes see babies. Their parents generally obtain my name from their friends, although several pediatricians, pediatric allergists, and a number of family physicians also send children to me. Children also come to me from primary schoolteachers and day-care-center staff who know of my work. Berkeley and its environs are psychologically oriented and child oriented, so it is not surprising that the practice of child psychotherapy would attract community interest. I have asked the various people who refer children to me (a) not to alarm parents and (b) not to refer for therapy but rather for a consultation about what seems to be bothering the child. I routinely perform fairly extensive consultations before taking a child into therapy.

THE DIAGNOSTIC CONSULTATION

The consultation consists of an initial meeting or two with the parents to obtain some idea of the current problem and to obtain a detailed developmental history, usually month by month over the child's life. I am particularly interested in (a) conditions during pregnancy and parturition, (b) feeding, (c) locomotion patterns in the infant, (d) attachment to and separations from the mother and cuddly toys or security blankets, (e) the range of emotional expressivity of the infant, (f) medical conditions, (g) developmental milestones, such as walking, weaning, speech development, (h) socialization patterns with other children, and (i) reactions to major changes, such as the beginning of school. I might inquire into general patterns of parental relationship from the point of view of the parental moods to which the infant was exposed. I also obtain the names and telephone numbers of all the other major caretakers, such as baby-sitters, day-care providers, teachers, and other relatives, so that I can obtain collateral views of the child in addition to the parents' own views. I also obtain birth and pediatric records when I can.

I then see the child a few times, usually twice a week, in a playroom. Rather prominent in the room is a sand tray and by its side are wide shelves with a range of miniatures. Paper, pencils, and colored crayons are available in another part of the room. A dollhouse, also well equipped with miniatures, occupies the third wall of the room.

Many children spontaneously construct Worlds without any overt instruction from me. More agitated or anxious children are often best served by some simple invitation to "make a make-believe world" or to do a drawing game. I tend to be fairly reticent and not especially active, which places a good deal of the initiative with the child. I try to sense what emotional distance I should adopt in relation to the child, varying this through each session as my sense dictates. During these few consultation sessions, I record both the child's and my reactions, and the play that emerges between us. I note both the content of the play and its articulation over the course of the session. I may talk a little with the child,

comment on the play, or ask gentle questions as to what is hap-
pening (in the child's view) in the play. I do not generally make
interpretations even on an exploratory basis during the consultation.

After three or four such sessions, I make another appointment
with the parents to discuss the child's reactions to the exposure to
the play situation, and to present my own, often quite tentative
conclusions about the child's personality structure and development. The brief intervention with the child in the consultation
quite often begins to show therapeutic effects on the child's mood,
and this is a favorable prognostic sign. I occasionally make a
recommendation for treatment, if I can see clear indications that
therapy would be beneficial, but usually I leave it to the parents to
conclude the possible benefits of play treatment, based on their
observations of their child's reactions to the consultation.

I tend to see children once or twice a week for a few months to a
few years. I see parents once or twice a month, both to report on
the course of treatment and to obtain reports from them on the
child's day-to-day life at home.

These procedures were followed in the two protocols presented
in Chapter 6. I present these cases, chosen from the large number
available to me, because they most clearly show the emergence of a
new theme in the child's play—the reparative motif—that appears
to mark an important change in the child's way of viewing the
world. This change seems so profound as to be legitimately regarded as a change in the balance of the internalizations in the
character structure. These conclusions are drawn in more detail in
the analysis of the data.

The cases were chosen for their special theoretical and clinical
significance. The information presented is quite selective, even
within the records of the play of each of the children. Presentation
of the entire protocol would be prohibitively detailed and extensive.
The selection was made to present a representative idea of the
general course of therapy. More detailed aspects of the play are
included as the moment approaches when the reparative motif is
about to emerge. I begin with a brief mention of my own level of
activity and restraint.

In these instances, as in almost all of the children I see, I tend to maintain a somewhat quiet and pensive presence, and I find myself fairly often "lost in thought" (this phrase is the closest description of my state that I can give). I am not particularly active, but this is not a forced inactivity; I am spontaneously quiet, although there are moments or even hours of more active involvement with some children. The cases I present are typical of my participation; I tended to observe and record the child's play, occasionally asking tentative questions. My involvement is not restricted to this level, however. There are profound nondiscursive aspects of the child-therapist interaction, which will be discussed later in the analysis of the data, insofar as they can be elaborated in words.

Quite rarely I might make tentative interpretations, but I have found classical interpretations less and less part of my therapeutic armamentarium. Occasionally, I will initiate the play with a suggestion that the child might make a World or tell a story, but only rarely. Generally I let the child set the pace and the theme of the play.

6
The First Case: Jennifer

THE CONSULTATION DATA

Both parents of this child are attorneys and were referred to me by a mutual friend in the mental health profession. I learned later that the person who made the referral had known it was necessary for some months but had waited until she sensed that the parents were ready and accessible to the suggestion that they might benefit from a consultation. The presenting complaint was that Jennifer, then aged 5½ years, was isolated and friendless at school; she would spend the lunch hour, normally a time when groups of children get together, fearfully clutching her best friend, her lunchbox. At home she was defiant, petulant, and moody; she also had extensive food fads, to the extent that her mother would cook separate meals for Jennifer—usually eggs, one of the few things she would eat.

The extra efforts put forward for Jennifer by her mother had become impossible on the birth of a new child, a son, some four months before she sought help. I recall that in the mother's initial consultation (she was alone) she was mortified by guilt and self-recrimination, which I have come to expect, particularly in mothers, but still find troubling. I briefly explained that these matters are usually more complex than whether any particular individual is doing or is not doing the "right thing" and that the particular developmental course of Jennifer's life would probably help us to understand her current predicament. I try to convey a development-centered approach, rather than a child- or family-centered approach; what this involves will be elaborated on in this protocol and in the subsequent discussion.

Jennifer was born when her father was 28 and her mother 27.

The parents had known one another for four years and had been married for two years at the time she was born. Birth was at full term after an uneventful pregnancy; delivery took place at the University of California Medical Center in San Francisco, a teaching hospital with an excellent reputation. Although Lamaze training had been undertaken, the labor lasted 30 hours and was completed with forceps. No anesthetic was used until late in the delivery, when a paracervical block was used. At birth Jennifer had good vital signs and was of good color. She stayed with her mother for only 20 minutes and was then taken to the nursery for the night.

Jennifer became demanding soon after birth and needed to be cared for and held a great deal. She had colic every evening from 5 P.M. to 11 P.M., and in the mother's words, "Nothing would make her happy except nursing. I nursed her every hour. I came to feel I was being eaten up."

At that time the father was taking the California bar examination and was quite occupied by his studies. He passed the examination, and the mother then went to law school, leaving Jennifer in her father's care in the daytime from the time she was 3 months old until she was 7 months old. Jennifer's reaction to this transition was not noted. Jennifer was placed in part-time day care at 7 months. Her mother felt that Jennifer had "much trouble separating" then, and this had continued to the present.

At 1 year Jennifer fell down six steps in a rocker but was uninjured. At 3 years she again fell down some stairs but was not hurt. By the age of 1 year Jennifer was already showing a "Jekyll and Hyde" personality. She would be really happy one moment and an "incredibly obnoxious child I [the mother] would want to strangle" the next. Bloch (1978), echoing Klein (see, for example, Klein 1927), refers to the child's fear of parental murderous rage, although she does not address the possible determinants in the child of these parental emotional states. Nevertheless, her presentation of the influence of the child's fantasy life is one of the closest to my thesis in the literature.

Jennifer's speech began at 1 year, and phrases were spoken by 2½ years. Toilet training was fairly slow; day training was achieved by 3 years and night training by 4½ years. For the six months prior to the consultation Jennifer had awakened at night with "bad dreams" about witches, robbers, and monsters. She sucked her thumb constantly and said that she did not like herself. When she looked at herself in the mirror, she would say, "That does not look like me," and also "does not feel like me" either.

Both parents felt "pushed to emotional extremes" in their attempts to be effective parents for Jennifer.

During the consultation I generally make some observations to myself about both the content and organization of the parents' descriptions of their child's developmental history. This may come to reflect the general atmosphere the family has adopted after struggling to deal with a traumatic situation involving the parents and the child in some form of unsatisfying or even embattled relationship.

Before reviewing the progression of Jennifer's play as she presented it to me, I will briefly review the presuppositions with which I approach the child's expressive play.

PRESUPPOSITIONS ABOUT THE CHILD'S EXPRESSIVE PLAY

In a child's mind there are depths and intensities of imagination that escape most adult minds. The nature and content of the child's imaginings are partly accessible to us through observation of the child's play in its richest, most expressive moments. But even play in children is much of the time only a feeble reflection of their inner world of experience. This inner drama, which continues in the child's awake and dreaming times, is the fantasy life of the child.

It is not clear to what extent a child may be able to be electively conscious of this fantasy life. Perhaps some of these imaginings are hidden even from the child, whereas others might occupy the child's complete attention. Certainly some children appear to be so preoccupied with their fantasy life that they may have little interest to give to external reality. This may prevent the child from attending to his or her own parents; it may impair the child's ability to invest energy and curiosity in learning; and it may prevent what we might regard as the natural attachment to other children in friendships. It is as though the fascinations of the inner drama attract so much of the child's concern that there is little else that seems important.

There is a body of theoretical knowledge that makes certain predictions about the content, organization, and progressive development of the fantasy life of children. This body of knowledge will be omitted from consideration at this time in order to allow Jennifer's stories to unfold and thus to speak for themselves. The stories were produced more or less spontaneously by Jennifer with little intervention from me. Initially, however, I had invited her to create a "make-believe world," and I had offered to write down anything she wanted to tell me about her make-believe world. I also offered to sketch any scenes she created with her toys.

PLAY SESSIONS

Selected extracts from Jennifer's play sessions are presented here in chronological sequence. In this protocol, the extracts consist of narrative descriptions of Jennifer's play, as she told them to me at the time, with my descriptions of her nonverbal play.

Session 1

A large hill is molded in the sand. A well is placed elsewhere in the scene. A small furry koala bear is at the top of the hill. The koala bear has only one wish. He wishes he had a friend.

Session 2

Jennifer molds the sand into shapes that my mind immediately associates with breast shapes; these molds are illustrated in Figure 12.

Extra sand is added to make the shape larger and larger. I asked, "Is that a breast?" Jennifer replied, "A what?" I repeated, "A

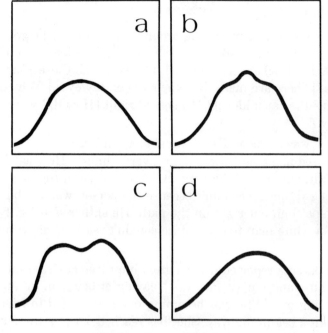

Figure 12. A mountain.

breast, like Mummy has." (I knew that her mother was currently breast-feeding her younger brother.) Jennifer replied, "No, it's a mountain."

Session 3

The little girl visits a magic hill with a well on top. The hill is surrounded on three sides by a stream where a horse goes to drink. The people live in a house and the horse lives in a barn. The wheels all came off their car and they have to go for a new car. They don't want their car because the wheels came off. The guy fixed it already, but they think it (the engine) may fall out again so they want a new car.

They look and look and look until they find a great new car, a yellow one. (But will it break down too?) They struggle to find a lady who will fit in the car. The daddy fits in easily, but we cannot seem to find a lady who will fit in the car.

Session 4

There was this guy driving around the roads but he got trapped. Getting buried was the trap. He's hidden. There's an X mark where he is buried. I'll show you. Close your eyes. [There are many Xs when I open my eyes.] Which X has the car under it? [I guessed right.] How did you know?!

There was a snake. He was real slow and lazy. He slithered along and was hungry, very hungry. He was gobbling up one of the persons [represented in the play by marbles], but he couldn't because the person was too big. He spat him out right on the path. He slithered along. He had a white man to eat, but he couldn't really swallow him.

The parents reported here "a great improvement"; Jennifer was less whiny and clingy and was "playing at being an infant more than being one." She was becoming more connected to friends at school in a beginning way. She "has reached out to grown-ups for the first time in her life," and she now slept peacefully at night.

Session 8

Jennifer seemed morose; her mother was in a good mood as she left Jennifer with me. Jennifer made pictures in the sand for me to guess. They were cookies. She fed me "cookies," "coffee," and "milk" from little plates and cups. She seemed very hurt when I said I had had enough to eat.

Session 10

I'm eating everything in the world, I'm just starving. "Momma, I have to go find my pet. She's so hungry." "Oh, honey, I don't want you eating any more." "I'm still *hungry!*" "I don't want you to get fat."

"Momma, I'm so starved, I'll eat *you* if you call me fat. I'll eat our house at home. [I'll eat us out of house and home?] Momma, I just found a bologna sandwich and ate it up. A big lump bumped into me."

Session 11

Scene 1. Four pigs are eating: two big ones, two little ones. They are all eating happily together.

Scene 2. Four monsters are all eating the snake. One said, "I like the tail, it's the juiciest." They are named

> Burgie the burglar monster
> Adeline the aggie monster
> Hairy the hairline monster
> Uggie the bug monster

Scene 3 (part sung).

Dig, dig, dig those roads. I think you are all being a wreck. Bump a dum. Why, he made a *new road*! We must dig a new road. That's the greatest idea, mister. Everybody who doesn't know the shortcut won't know there's a new road. I think you're all being silly about this. There's going to be no new road. Just banks and cities.

We're making a new world now. Why, a new world! [In amazement] Everybody come away. Get out of the way, come on, everybody. Everybody go bye-bye. We're having new roads.

Come to see the wonderful show. Oh, ho ho. Bo bo. They've seen a band.

Session 12

Jennifer molded the sand into a hill and placed jewels on top of it (see Figure 13). She told the following story:

The dinosaurs live at the bottom of the mountain. They want the jewels from the top of the hill. The jewels just

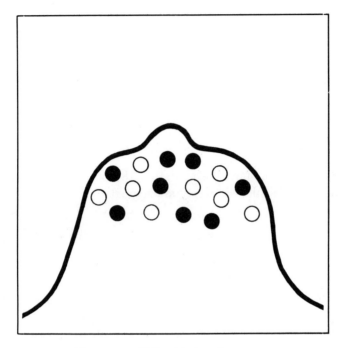

Figure 13. Hill with jewels on top.

appear. They're magic. The mountain grew there by magic where the jewels are. The dinosaurs take the jewels down, but the next morning the biggest dinosaur notices the hill has disappeared. Once you take the jewels from the hill, it would go down.

The Indians come. They fight the dinosaurs. Then one night some more people come. When the Indians came out of their hiding place, the other people were all over, just walking around. Then the different dinosaurs, one came out and helped the little people fight the Indians. Then the dinosaur had forgotten all about the jewels, so he runs to his house and gets his jewels and runs to his friend's house and gets theirs.

The Indians want all the jewels, and they kill the dinosaurs and the other people. Then they get the jewels.

The Indians came from another place because they heard about the jewels.

The following sessions are verbatim transcripts of the stories Jennifer told about her sand play.

Session 13

Once there was a snake living on a rock. One day he got tired of grazing in the sun on the rock and he slithered off the rock and followed the path. Then he kept on traveling and traveling until he came to the flattest place in the world. He was hungry and slithered along to see if there was anything to eat.

He came across the glass container and opened the door. Then he saw a little person running down the hall. He said, "That's what I'll have for lunch." So he opened up his mouth and the little person, by mistake, ran right into it. Then he tried to chew. He chewed and chewed and chewed. Then the little person slipped out, fell out, and the little person ran away.

The little person stopped and pretended to be dead. The snake slithered off to him and sniffed and listened to the person. Then he opened his mouth and chewed and chewed, and before he knew it his teeth were rotten and the little person was in his stomach. Then he growled, "Yum, yum, yum." Then he yawned and said, "There's no rock to sleep on." So with his tail he scratched lots of the dirt and made a dirt rock. Then he slithered on top and fell fast asleep.

Next morning he woke up bright and early. He yawned and said, "What about breakfast?" Then he slithered over, sniffing and looking for the glass container, remembering the last night and the little person. He saw hundreds of little people so he opened his mouth and the two twins ran in by mistake. He said, "One person is enough, the other I will save for lunch." Then he opened up his mouth wide and gulped and chewed one. His teeth went so deep down that he couldn't get them out. He pulled and chewed and finally he went kerplunck.

Then the twins ran out and ran and ran and couldn't run anymore, so he played like he was dead. Then the little snake listened to his heart and heard it was beating. Before he knew it his teeth were rotted up. Besides that, the little person was in his stomach. So he slithered along and was still hungry. He was sniffing to see what he could eat. He made a path as he went along. Suddenly he stood up and smelled some young persons. He noticed a little guy running and playing. The snake opened his mouth. But the guy was too tough.

Session 14

Once upon a time there lived a koala bear. The koala bear was trapped behind a fence. One day he noticed there was no other fence so he took a big leap and jumped. He landed over the fence. Well, he was so happy that he ran and he jumped. He clapped his hands and his feet. He took the fence, climbed onto it, and threw it away. It landed on the man who had trapped him, and then the man hopped on his motorbike and went "B-R-R-R" and drove all the way back to where the koala bear was. "Ah ha!" he said, parking his motorcycle. "Now I've got you." He pulled out of his pocket the fence. He said, "Don't move, you thing," and the koala bear stood right where he was.

The man took one fence and put around the side of the koala bear. "Oh no!" said the koala bear, but he knew he could jump over the fences. He was just tricking the man. The man took another piece of fence and put that on the other side. "Oh no, oh no, oh no!" said the little koala bear. The man put on another piece of fence. "Oh no, oh no! No no no no no!" said the koala bear. The man put on the last piece of fence. "Oh no, oh no, oh no, no no!" said the koala bear. Now he had fences all around him. The man locked the gate by pressing the dirt all up around the fences to lock the gate and trap the koala bear.

The gate was cold and squishy. Then the koala bear was so frightened he jumped up and down and up and down and said, "Oh no, oh no, oh no! I just have to make it." He made a big jump and a right turn and landed on the ground. "Oh boy, I made it!" he said, and he jumped on the man's motorbike, squishing it. He broke the fence and carried it back to where it belonged in the man's pocket.

The man came back, and when he noticed that the koala bear was just hanging in the tree looking down at him, laughing at him, the man was so angry he jumped up and down and squished the motorbike some more. He got so furious that he rode his bike all the way home.

Session 15

Once upon a time there lived two little kids called the Lollipop Kids. They loved to do little dances about themselves and they lived in a little house. So they ran outside of the house and then one of them said, "Let's do a dance of ourselves." "Okey dokey," said the other one.

Each put their hands on top of their head and danced, singing," "We are the Lollipop Kids." They moved their heads up and down, they moved their arms back and forth, and they moved their legs here and there and did little wiggles, singing, "We are the Lollipop Kids who live all alone."

They decided they didn't want to do any more dances. They played roll the dice. One of them got "out." So they decided to play another game. So they ran around and the person who stopped first, won. Then one of them said, "I don't want to play games anymore. I want to be a big kid and go to school." "Okay, you can go to school but I will stay a little kid and play games," said the other.

The kid who went to school had to sit in the seat all

day long and do reading and writing all day long. He had
to learn the whole alphabet and to learn his numbers from
one to one hundred. One day he said, "I do not like school.
I want to go back to be a baby, to play games with my
sister." He ran over the hills and the green grass. He
finally found his hut. Well, well, well. His sister was
playing sliding along the grass. Pretty soon she got tired of
that and ran to balance on the balancing wheel.

"Hi, sister, I'm back." "Hi, brother. Why are you back?"
said the sister. "It was too hard," said the brother. "I had
to do too much work but I learned how to count up to
five." "How do you count up to five?" said the sister, who
was surprised he had learned one little thing. "It goes like
this: One, one, two, two, three, three, four, four, five, five.
Okay, you try it by yourself, sister." "One, two, four, five."
"You skipped three! I also learned the alphabet up to E."
"How does that go?" "A, B, C, D, E. I had to stay at
school to learn that." "Oh boy, I'd like to go to school to
learn that," said the sister. "You'll be sorry," said the
brother, calling off to her.

She went running over the hills and the green grass
until she came to the school. "Oh boy, I might learn up to
Z this time," she cried, running to see her numbers and
letters.

"Oh, you're back," said the teacher. "No, I'm his sister," she
said. So the teacher said, "You may sit at this desk." The little
girl sat down and she sat writing this and reading that,
counting to five and six and seven and eight, doing her letters
A and B and C and D and E and F and G and H and all
the letters. One day at recess she said, "This is too hard
for me" and ran back to her brother.

"I learned the whole alphabet and the numbers up to
twenty," said the sister. "And guess what I even did. I
learned how to read all the books except the real long
ones." "Please tell me the whole alphabet," he said.
"ABCDEFGHIJKLMNOPQRSTUVWXYZ," she said. "Why,
that's great!" he said in amazement. "Now tell me up to

twenty!" he cried. So she counted one, two, three all the way
up to twenty. "Wow!" he cried. "I'm going to use you to
remind me when I go back to school."

They both ran back to school. Finally it was summer
vacation for them and sadly both ran back home. "Well, at
least that was fun."

Session 16

This session should be read closely since it shows the emergence
of the reparative motif in two forms: the solution of desperate
(infantile) hunger and the solution of Jennifer's contemporary
loneliness.

Once upon a time Harry Hublick was slithering along and
growling because he was hungry. Then he found a feast of
food. He said, "Yum, yum, that looks like lunch," and he
gobbled it down. Suddenly Druple Purple came along. "Hi,"
said Harry. "Hi," said Druple Purple. "Aren't you hungry?"
said Druple Purple. "No, I just ate some food," said Harry.
"Well, I am," said Druple Purple. "Then just keep on
digging and you may find some," said Harry.

They dug and dug and dug and dug. "I can't find any,"
said Druple Purple [exasperated voice]. "Well, we'll just
have to keep looking," said Harry Hublick. So they dug
some more. Pretty soon Druple Purple said, "I can't find
it."

Just then Scaley Raley came walking down. "What are
you doing?" he said to Harry Hoplick and Druple Purple.
"We're looking for food," said Druple Purple. "Well, I may
help you," said Scaley Raley. So they all searched together.
They searched and searched and searched for the food.
Suddenly Scaley Raley found some food. "Oh boy, oh boy,
oh boy, oh boy!" he yelled. "What was it?" said Harry
Hoplick. "What, what?" said Druple Purple. "I found some
food," he said, and put it down on the ground. "Slurp!" said
Druple Purple. He was slurping up the food. Druple

Purple was starved to death. So Scaley said, "No, no, no! It's mine. I found it and I get it."

"I got an idea," said Harry Hopeless. "We'll share it. First you take a bite, but if you take two bites you won't get any," said Harry. "You take one bite, then I'll take a teeny tiny bite (because I had lunch already), then Druple Purple can take the rest." "Harolyn Hopeless will take a teeny tiny bite because he's not that hungry. He just had lunch." Then Scaley Raley took one bite. "Crunch!" Then Harolyn Hopeless bit a teeny corner off. "Krop!" Then Druple Purple ate the rest. "Krop!" Then it was all done. "Yummy, yummy," said Druple Purple. "Shlurp!" said Scaley Raley. "Haaaaah!" said Harolyn Hopeless.

"Let's all sing a song," said Scaley Raley. "I'm not good at singing," said Druple Purple. "I don't feel like it," said Harolyn Hopeless. "Well, I do," said Scaley Raley. So he sang and sang and sang until he couldn't sing anymore. Pretty soon Druple Purple and Harolyn Hopeless were tired of hearing him singing so they dug their hands under the sandy ground, plugged their ears by putting their head under between their hands.

But he sang and danced. "La la la la la. Oh, ho ho," he sang and danced. "Da da da da da." So very soon he stopped singing. They came out of their sand and cried, "Are you done singing?" Scaley Raley said, "Yep, let's all go dance to a record player." "I don't feel like it," said Purple Druple. "I'm not very good at it," said Harolyn Hopeless. "Well, I want to," said Scaley Raley, skipping over to turn on the record player. He turned on the switch and danced until he could dance no more.

Purple Druple and Harolyn Hopeless soon got tired of watching. So they buried their eyes in the sand. So he danced and he danced until he could dance no longer. Pretty soon he turned off the record player so they took out their blurred eyes. And then he said, "Well well well, my my my, wouldn't you like to gather in the fields?"

"I know you'll say no," said Scaley Raley, "so why don't
I do it by myself?" "No no no no no no!" they cried. "Our
eyes have stopped getting tired of listening to you sing. No,
we'll go out and play in the fields with you." He jumped,
"Yippee!" and so did Harolyn Hopeless and Purple Druple.

Session 17

In this session Jennifer's acceptance of her own constructive
aggression continues.

Once upon a time there lived a little boy called the Lollipop
Kid. He had no mummy or daddy. He was just left in a
mean old forest that had the meanest, baddest dinosaur
that ever lived. But he didn't know there was a mean, bad
dinosaur because he was too young to understand when
they would talk and worry about him.

The time went by and he played along the banks and
hardly ever saw the orange demon scraping past him. It
was really the meanest monster in the West. So he played
and one day the half-boy, half-girl whatever was playing
over the hills in the green grass when he noticed a big sort
of orange demon coming towards him. He said, "Hi, Mr.
Demon. What are you doing today?"

Mr. Demon began to growl and grouch. Then he began
to charge towards the little boy. "I'm sorry, mister. What is
your name?" said the little boy, petting his scaley back.
"KHHHHHHHHHR," said the demon. "I really do not have
a name. You must forgive me because everyone hates me
just because I'm scary. I'm really the nicest dinosaur." The
little boy said, "You're so cute I think I'm going to use you
for a pet." So he hopped on the back of the orange demon,
who he called Mr. Demon, and rode off.

"So, Mr. Demon," he said, "how have you been? Are you
lonely so far since everyone runs away from you?" The

wicked old scaley dragon said, "Yes, I am. Everyone will be surprised because they see someone on my back."

So they growled and grunched through the forest. Pretty soon the scaley orange demon stopped for a drink of water. "What are you doing?" said the Lollipop Kid, crouching down beside him. "Slurp!" he said, with a loud gulp. "Slurp, I'm thirsty. Now, I am hungry. Want to join me?"

"Yes, I would," said the Lollipop Kid, crouching down to drink some water and get some food wherever it was. "Now for the food," said the scaley orange demon. "I'm hungry, aren't you?" "I doubt there will be anything done when I'm left," he said, smacking his lips. "Well, why don't you just go ahead and eat." "Where's the food?" said the Lollipop Kid. "Right here," said the dinosaur. "Just come a little closer and you can see it." So the Lollipop Kid ran over to see it and suddenly, "KR-CRUNCH! CHOMP, CHOMP, CHOMP! Isn't that good?" he said. But the boy didn't answer because his leg was eaten off. Everybody was so scared of the scaley demon because he was a man-eater.

"Why, you! I'm not scared of you, I'm just mad at you. I thought you said you were going to be my friend," said the boy, hopping on one foot. "But I'm still hungry," said the dinosaur, smacking his lips for another leg. And, "KR-CRUNCH! GULP, GULP, GULP!" And another "KR-CRUNCH! GULP, GULP, GULP!" And another "KR-CRUNCH! GULP, GULP, GULP!" And another leg was gone. The boy fell flat on his butt. "Now look what you've done. I can't even stand now. Are you going to eat my whole body?" "Yes, I am," the dinosaur said, smacking his lips for one arm.

And when the boy tried to get the arm away, the scaley monster pulled and tugged on it hard. But he could not get his teeth into the boy's arm. The boy pulled it up and poked the teeth into the monster's gum and did it with all the teeth so they weren't there anymore. So then he pulled out his arm and then he pulled out his two legs from the monster's belly. And then he put them back again and he kicked the monster. The monster got all curled up. His legs were twisted round and round, and then they were twisted on top of him and his tail was curled into a little ball. He himself was all tangled up into the smallest ball imaginable in the world. So the boy climbed onto his back and said, "There'll never be a scaley dinosaur demon orange monster again."

ANALYSIS OF JENNIFER'S PLAY

This analysis will be conducted in two parts. First, there will be a more general view of the overall direction of the course of treatment, followed by a more specific examination of the play protocol as it reflects aspects of Jennifer's internal experience. Part of the analysis will be reserved for a comparative study of both children in the discussion.

The Overall Course of the Play Themes

It will have been observed that in the stories historical and contemporary reality are presented concurrently. The theme of not having any friends is interposed in the early (first four) sessions with the themes of primitive orality, of feeling immobilized (the car without any wheels, without an engine), and of being trapped or stuck. When Jennifer turned to me to find hidden elements of the scene, she reflected her first understanding, at some level, that she could (a) use me in her play, and more symbolically (b) use me to find aspects of herself she had hidden. This aspect will also be seen in the protocol presented in the next chapter.

The scenes continue the themes of hunger and stasis, but more primitive aspects emerge, both in the intensity of the drive ("I'm starving!") and of the play symbol (e.g., the use of monsters known to populate her bad dreams). During the therapy hour, Jennifer seems more conflicted, distressed, animated, and suffering. I do not find myself enjoying the sessions; in fact I appear to be feeling more rootless, discouraged, and concerned as the play progresses in its primitive direction. Concurrent with the morbid themes, however, the play becomes increasingly organized, and there are intercessions of more optimistic themes, particularly the "new world" theme of session 11.

The scenes become more animated and diverse, with more overt movement in the themes and (in session 12) the idea that there are "other places" from which people (or monsters) can come. In other words, there is a progressive release from ego constriction, allowing "new" ideas to enter Jennifer's mind. These scenes are preparatory to the long, complicated, and thematically central stories, beginning with session 13, which have a compelling quality to them and which are of a quite different emotional tone. These stories describe a problem (as fairy stories often do) and provide the solution within the same story. The child has discovered a method with which to link the frightening or otherwise traumatic initial idea in the story with a more "giving" or reassuring aspect within his or her imagination. The child also introduces elements of humor so that both therapist and child can enjoy the session with playful and more mature exchanges.

At the point of transition there is an observable shift in the child's sublimatory ability (see the much greater length and complexity of the later stories), indicating an improvement in the degree to which the child can invest formerly trapped libido in the therapeutic task—that is, in the service of the developing ego. It is the absence of this ability that is thought to contribute to the fixation in the original infantile instance.

In particular it will be observed that many of the images used in these "reparative" stories are culled from previous sessions. It is as if the child were initially teaching the therapist the language of her own unconscious in order to be able to share with the therapist the reparative task and the therapeutically generated reparative scenes.

The significance of this "linguistic education" of the therapist will be considered in the discussion. These rather general aspects of the play do not adequately explain the mental origins of some of the play themes, and these will be considered in more detail.

Analysis of Early Play Sessions

The simplicity and lack of recordable play in the first session are explicable partly through Jennifer's fears of this new situation and her fear of me. There is some exploratory play with the sand, molding and sifting it, and much wandering around the room. In the absence of any direction from me, the determinants of Jennifer's mentation become intrapsychic, and she reflects both her own sense of disconnectedness and her wish for me to be the missing friend. I would later come to see the type of disconnectedness as being protective, designed to avoid the ravages of oral need and oral aggression, both of which threaten annihilation of the child or of the other. It is unclear to me what moved me to want to identify Jennifer's mountain as "a breast," nor is its therapeutic significance evident. It might be that this intervention precipitated the "drinking" theme of the next session.

The themes in session 3 become more interwoven and complex in their determinants. There is an initial statement of the play situation and the transference relationship. Jennifer is visiting a "magical" reconstruction of her mother's breast in the play. There is the motif of damage and possible repair or replacement. But we do not know if the new car will be any better than the first.

There are many possible meanings to Jennifer's difficulty in "finding a lady who will fit into the car." There is an abundance of miniatures of both sexes, but there is a psychological prohibition in Jennifer on finding a well-fitting lady. I think it is also significant that whereas the man is a "daddy," the missing woman is a "lady" rather than a "mummy." My own best interpretation of the meaning of this part of the story lies in the differential relationships that children with early developmental fixations establish with each parent.

The mother seems much more to be a vehicle for the problematic infantile themes (in this case the oral-incorporative-destructive theme) and for their resolution in the child's mind. It was at the mother's breast that love and hate were first experienced. Later in life the remnants of symbiotic attachment tend to make mothers and their children much more emotionally involved at a primitive level than fathers and their children. This factor can lead parents to have quite dissonant perceptions of one and the same child and can even lead to friction as to which view should prevail. There are, however, speculative interpretations of this material, for I have not fully consciously understood Jennifer's play language.

In session 4 a double motif emerged. There is the clear statement of the blocking of aggressive libido: "This man's driving and he gets trapped. He's hidden." Similarly, Jennifer's own driving, outgoing, aggressive libido, which she could have used to face life's challenges, was itself trapped in a hidden part of her personality. The second motif contains a reassuring and terrifying paradox. I will assume that in the first statement the snake again reflects Jennifer herself in her fantasmic relationship with me, and that I represent to her an internal object, presumably the "breast" (this presumption is based on the statement that the snake is "very very hungry"). The snake is prevented from destroying the "white man" because he (the man) is too big, but it also means that the snake will remain very, very hungry.

This paradox captures Jennifer's problem in establishing any relationship with friends. To her the hunger for a friend is felt to be consumingly and dangerously strong, threatening the friend; on the other hand, she herself is threatened by her continuing craving for relatedness. We might already be able to formulate the idea that Jennifer's detachment is caused by a fantasy she has of the destructiveness of her oral need and aggression. In reality her clinging dependency indeed drove others away, and it infuriated her parents. In this picture the way in which the child's worst fantasy is translated into the reality of the mother-child relationship becomes painfully clear. Rather than risk this threat, Jennifer "spits out" the wished-for friends.

My consultation with the parents after this fourth session showed the quite predictable, symptomatic improvement that young children in play therapy show as the play takes over from the parental relationship the function of expressing and containing the child's dominant infantile conflicts.

In session 8 there is probably a technical error on my part when I declined more of the imaginary cookies, claiming to be satisfied. I had not understood the language well enough, nor had I followed my usual inclinations to let the child dictate the play without my resisting the theme in any way. In fact, I brought Jennifer up short with my statement that I was satisfied. I became disconnected from the fantasy place I actually occupied as her starving self, or more accurately, as the part of herself that was starving. The theme not surprisingly intensified in the next reported session, session 10. ("I'm eating everything in the world.") At this point a startling transformation begins to occur. Previously masked themes become simplified and made more primitive.

Session 11 shows the degree of splitting between benign and hungry aspects of Jennifer's personality. In the benign first scene, pigs are eating. This is followed by the monsters (this is the first mention or use of monsters), lasciviously chewing on a snake. After expressing this split, Jennifer goes on to speak about the need for a new road and a new world. We could see this in the interpretive schema described in Chapter 3: the expressed need for a missing bridge between these opposing percepts of the eating process, as a form of intuitive knowledge. The expression of the split and the *child's* suggestion for a transitional motif represents the onset of what I have termed the reparative motif.

The reparative motif occurs after and in response to the child's statement of the intrapsychic dilemma. It contains the suggestion of reconciling opposites or of fulfilling previously unmet, primitive needs. Even in this moment of promise, however, there are cynical and depressive elements: "I think you're just being silly about this. There's going to be no new road." But the positive theme persists, and in her first moment of disinhibited glee Jennifer sings a little song.

The reparative motif brings considerable relief to the child as soon as it is devised. The subsequent stories become much more elaborate, and they show a remarkable degree of coherent organization. It should be remembered that these stories were spontaneously created by the child without any addition of material by the therapist and that they are presented directly as they were recorded during the child's telling of them. I will allude to this extraordinary manifestation of cognitive organization in the discussion.

In session 12 two themes begin to merge. The monsters theme and the treasure theme are linked. The jewels, which magically make the hill grow and in their absence disappear, seem to represent a new motif, that of precious contents. We can at the least attribute to the jewels the meaning of "good objects."

This theme reflects quite directly Jennifer's idea that if one takes good things (jewels) from their source (the mountain), then it will be destroyed. Translated to her own early experience: if one takes too much milk from the breast, it will be destroyed or depleted. Put in terms of her contemporary relationships, contaminated as they were by these fantasies: if one accepts love from a friend, the friend will be destroyed.

In the next part of Jennifer's story (in session 12) there are two kinds of monsters and two kinds of people. Rather than splitting her perceptions into savage monsters and innocent people, Jennifer begins to see that aggression (the dinosaurs) can be used constructively. This story shows the beginnings of the integration of love and aggression. These beginnings gave Jennifer a new ability to think in more hopeful ways. It will be observed that subsequent stories show dramatic improvements in their organization, complexity, diversity, and richness. These cognitive steps reflect the changed availability of interest and concern inside Jennifer: rather than being bound up in a neurotic preoccupation, the energy is released for investment in cognitive exercises.

Prereparative Themes

In session 13 there is a struggle between a hungry snake and a "little person." In the story the snake suffers from "rotting teeth" after his attack on the little person. The story ends with the comment that the "guy was too tough" (for the snake to chew up). We have the sense that the little guys have survived in spite of the hungry snake's attack. Jennifer no longer needs to fear the attacks made on her by her own inner (angry) hunger. The hunger remains, but it is not felt to be so dangerous.

Session 14 contains an interlude story that interrupts the sequence of hunger themes. The story is about a fenced-in koala bear. In play scenes fences are used to define and divide territory, to enclose or to shut out one part of the scene from another. They structure and regulate the scene. Consequently, I think of fence or cage scenes as analogs of the structuring processes in the child's mind. The child is illustrating inner regulating and sometimes constricting ("trapping") parts of the mind that influence the flow of the emotions.

The story of this session movingly portrays the koala's struggle for freedom, and his eventual triumph over the captor. "Oh boy, I made it!" the koala says as he overcomes his fright and leaps to freedom. This theme again shows Jennifer's new sense of her own courage. She now feels able to escape from her prison of fear.

Following this "liberation," Jennifer devises a playful, light-hearted story in which the two children take pleasure in learning their letters and numbers (session 15). Note the joke in the exchange between the teacher and the little girl: "You're back." "No, I'm his sister." The story and the session end on the note: "Well, at least that was fun."

The Emergence of the Reparative Motif

Session 16 contains an exemplary illustration of the child's development of a comprehensive reparative motif. The story opens with a starving monster "growling because he is hungry." The monster is seen as male, I think, to prevent Jennifer from recognizing herself as the hungry monster. Harry cannot find food, however hard he looks. He becomes hopeless, and his name actually changes to "Harolyn Hopeless." Purple Druple (pronounced Drurple) is even hungrier than Harolyn/Harry. Neither can find any food.

Scaley comes along and offers help: "Well, I may help you." Scaley soon finds some food and all three eat to satisfaction. Here we see the child's recruitment of a transitional theme (Scaley) to assist in an otherwise hopeless task; Purple was "starved to death" before Scaley came along. Jennifer has found in herself a link between her own lost "food," or sense of nurturance, and her own painful hunger. This link relieves her dangerous hunger.

Thereafter, the story turns to Jennifer's contemporary problem: friendlessness. Scaley attempts to befriend Harolyn and Purple with no success. He dances, he sings, but they ignore him. *Just as Scaley is about to give up,* as if by magic, Harolyn and Purple stop "being tired," and they join Scaley to play in the fields.

At another point of maximum desperation, then, when even Scaley is about to give up hope, a new reparative leap occurs. Both Jennifer's hunger and her isolation have been "solved" in play.

The following session, 17, demonstrates Jennifer's command and enjoyment of the exercise of the reparative motif. The hunger/affiliation themes have been addressed, but the persecution/ destruction incorporation theme has not. The Lollipop Kid (one of the twins) returns in a friendly disposition to an unfriendly monster. The extraordinary use of humor in this story maintains a light mood in the face of the frightening themes. When the demon has just bitten off his second leg, causing him to "fall on his butt," the Lollipop Kid turns to the monster and says, "Now look what you've done!" in a masterpiece of understatement. But the monster eventually succumbs to the Lollipop Kid's triumphant self-assertion. "Now there'll never be a scaley dinosaur demon orange monster again," he says, using the same name for the demon as for the hungry monster from the week before. A consolidation is made of the final laying to rest of the hungry demon inside Jennifer.

Some weeks later, after further similar themes moderating in their intensity and becoming more consistent in their reflection of the improved balance in her internal fantasies, Jennifer started to tell stories such as the following: "Once upon a time, there was some sand and the sand went squiggle, squoggle all around town. One day the sand said, 'The End,' and that's the end of the story." Later in the same session (which actually was session 26), another story ended thus: "And then he said, 'Helicopter, you know what?'" and he yelled in the helicopter's ear, very loudly, 'THE END!' And that is the end."

I scheduled two further sessions and mentioned to Jennifer's parents that I thought it was time to stop. Although they were a little apprehensive, they agreed to end the treatment as I suggested, and I have continued to monitor through her schoolteachers Jennifer's continued progress in the subsequent four years.

These sessions have been analyzed in detail, not to show what happens in the therapist's mind during the treatment but rather to demonstrate the reflection in the play themes of the hypothesized mutative process of internal repair in the child's world of object relations. This child produced quite explicit stories about her sand play, which makes the illustration of the emergence of the reparative motif in its combined complexity and elegance relatively easy.

Following is another illustration in which the play took place at a less verbal level. This protocol requires more inferential judgment of the play themes, which may not be easy unless the reader is familiar with the processes of inferential reasoning commonly used in depth-psychology analysis of associative processes. Nevertheless, using the first child to introduce the concept, I show the evolution of the reparative motif in a different child with quite different personality dynamics.

7
The Second Case: Christine

THE CONSULTATION DATA

Christine, an 8-year-old girl, was brought in with the following presenting symptoms. She was argumentative, defiant over even the slightest matters, and given to periods of suicidal despair in which she would say she wished she were dead. She was petulant and attacked her younger sister and stepmother, apparently without provocation. She then would change abruptly into an affectionate mood, would become apologetic, and would say she did not know what had come over her. In school and in extracurricular activities Christine was easily discouraged; she felt unable to manage unfamiliar or challenging tasks and would quickly give up in despair.

Christine's parents were married when both were 18, reportedly after receiving a false-positive pregnancy test result. They had been childhood sweethearts. Immediately after the marriage, Christine's mother, Joan, conceived again. During the pregnancy (it is not clear at what stage), Joan "jumped on a fence and fell down on her stomach," and at seven months there was slight bleeding. Delivery was at term and the baby was in good health, labor having been only six hours. Christine was breast-fed for six weeks and then breast-feeding was discontinued, although I do not know the reason for this change.

The parents separated many times after Christine's birth. Her father, Alan, eventually left when Christine was 6 months old, and little is known of the next year of her life except that she was beaten by Joan's new boyfriend (although not by Joan herself). The courts eventually intervened on a petition by Alan, who was awarded custody. He had remarried, and Christine lived with him and his new wife to the present time.

For the first four months after this change in custody, Christine was withdrawn and unresponsive; she was not talking. Gradually she became more animated, but her animation consisted of screaming fits in which she would shout, "Mommy, Mommy!" constantly. She was also somnambulistic and had night terrors. She could not be awakened during her sleepwalking or terrors and had no memory of them subsequently.

Until she was 4, Christine banged her head against the walls and floors, to the point that "neighbors complained and wondered how her brain could survive." The father and the adoptive stepmother asked the advice of both their pediatrician and the supervising probation officer who was in charge of the custody. These professionals were said to have reassured the parents that Christine "would just grow out of it."

In spite of the history of physical abuse, Christine continued to visit her natural mother and her stepfather, and it is thought that the abuse continued. The courts intervened again, stipulating that the maternal grandparents would have to be present to supervise the visits. Christine's mother was very variable in her presence at these visits; in fact, Christine was usually staying with the grandparents and might sometimes see her mother then. Christine's natural mother had trouble with the law (she passed numerous bad checks), and her boyfriend was arrested and jailed for burglary. There was a report of Christine's having returned from a visit with a blurred story of what seemed to have been an incident of sexual abuse, but the details were not clear, and I could not confirm the actual events.

Although the history in this case is not as detailed as I would have liked (I was unable to obtain coherent information from the natural mother), certain features of the play are particularly revealing of this child's dynamic internal processes and illustrate well the evolution of therapeutic change.

THE PLAY SCENES

The scenes from Christine's play presented here consist of photographs of her World scenes with brief narrative descriptions.

Session 1

Scene 1. Two palm trees, one with one living and one dead branch, are seen in the center of an empty desert (see Figure 14).

Scene 2. An abandoned castle traps a white horse. Two cars and a train, apparently unconnected with the castle, are pointing away from the castle (see Figure 15).

Scene 3. A prehistoric scene is created in which cavemen are seen in various aggressive positions defending their caves. A saber-toothed tiger faces the caves. She has come to her cub whom the cavemen keep in one of their caves (see Figure 16).

Scene 4. I am asked to look away while the scene is prepared. After some minutes I am instructed to look at the scene (see (Figure 17). The sand appears blank. In fact, some 36 animals are buried. It is my task to find the missing animals. Then I have to hide the animals for Christine to find. She is extremely amused by this game.

Christine made all these scenes in her first hour; there was an air of frantic determination but businesslike efficiency in the way

Figure 14. Two palm trees.

Figure 15. An abandoned castle.

she put the scenes together. Subsequent scenes were produced with more care and pensiveness. Christine made very few comments on her World scenes. The descriptions below are my own unless otherwise stated.

Session 2

The session began with another "bury and find the animals" game. A little bunny watched the hide-and-seek game from a

Figure 16. A prehistoric scene.

Figure 17. Hide-and-seek game.

vantage point on the corner of the sand tray. After one turn each of being the "finder," Christine decided she wanted to make another World.

In Figure 18 we see that a diagonal line of paired animals is arranged from the left rear to the center of an otherwise deserted scene. At the front (near the center of the tray) is the little bunny, then a hen and a pig, two lambs, and a progression through two

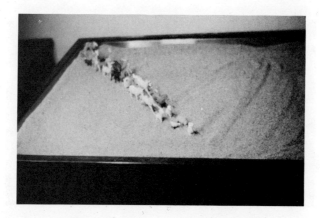

Figure 18. Procession of animals.

pairs of horses, two dogs, two reindeer, and two giraffes. A tiger (the saber-toothed tiger of the previous week) and a "ferocious lion" (her words) are at the back.

Christine's stepmother reports that she is no longer attacking her sister and instead is "playing with her." Except for continuing problems at bedtime, Christine is more cooperative and easygoing at home. This symptomatic improvement will be discussed in both its possible defensive and therapeutic aspects in the analysis and discussion.

Session 3

The sequence of animals from the week before was reconstructed in a modified form (see Figure 19). Rather than being in an empty expanse, the sequence was part of a picture that included the train and cars (from session 1) and a fenced-off oasis of trees. A lake with boats on it also occurs in this picture.

Session 4

In Figure 20, we see that the lion and the tiger from the back of the line have now come to be immediately behind the bunny and a chick. Two large cannons are placed near but pointing away from

Figure 19. Procession in context.

this foursome. The trees are no longer fenced; they surround the lake in a less confined way. The tree (from the first scene) is given a place of prominence near the folded fences. The train is coming to the front of the scene, but its way is barred by a closed train crossing, a parking sign, and (added last) a witch on a broomstick.

At that point Christine ran out of the room and entered the adjacent "wet" playroom where she made a picture. At the end of the painting she titled the picture "My hearts." Figure 21 shows a large, many-layered heart in a box surrounded by many tiny red (some almost dagger-shaped) hearts.

Session 5

A new scene is constructed in which there are two homes, each of which has a car, a boat, and a plane (see Figure 22). One house is conspicuously larger than the other. A road goes from the houses at the front center of the scene to a lake at the rear. There is a gas station where the cars have to go for gas at the rear. The road is blocked by an auto mechanic's ramp and by the closed rail crossing seen earlier. "The people can't go out to the lake because the road is blocked."

Figure 20. Complex scene.

Figure 21. "My hearts."

Session 6

The two-house motif is repeated with a fenced corral, containing horses, for each house (see Figure 23). A mysterious pair of knights has appeared, facing one another across double fences that separate the houses. A vacant "no-man's-land" is in the center of the scene; there are no roads. The larger house has several dogs; the other

Figure 22. The house theme.

Figure 23. "Your house and mine."

none. Christine tells me the smaller house belongs to me; the larger is hers.

It should be noted at this point that I have made no interpretations whatever to Christine in the course of the play, nor has she said more than the few remarks reported above to me. I am nonetheless satisfied that a special language of child-therapist communication is evolving. Christine also continues her dramatic symptomatic remission.

Session 7

Again we see the previous device of the creation of a scene with many organizing fences, which is then allowed to interact internally by the removal of the fences (cf. sessions 3 and 4). In Figure 24 the scene from the week before is animated, and for the first time Christine tells a little story: "The small house's horses are being attacked by a coyote. Their own dogs try to fight it off, but they can't. The horses are going to be killed." There is a moment of true desperation and panic. Then "the horses are saved because the dogs from the other house, from my house, come over and drive him away. Then he never comes back."

Figure 24. Reparative scene.

At this point I should mention that there was a sudden discontinuity in the emotional tone of the session and in my sense of this child. Whereas before she had appeared frightened, volatile, and vulnerable, she suddenly appeared confident, relieved, and held herself with a different and contrasting air. I have come to think of this moment as one when children begin to find in themselves a new strength and confidence wherein problems or frights, although real, can be psychologically overcome. This moment is moving and powerful in its impact on the therapist. There is a shared feeling that a terrifying nightmare that has been looming "somewhere" has taken a turn for the better.

For the sake of clarity, abbreviated notes are presented on the subsequent sessions.

Session 8

The World scene was a circus. Previously wild animals were captured and tamed. Lots of people came to watch them perform. The animals are kept in cages, segregated according to the type of animal. The scene is varied and full. The people enjoy the circus.

Christine is reported to be much calmer at home. Her nighttime defiance has ceased.

Session 10

Two Worlds are made. There is a circus in which the horses are called, "Fearless," "Fierce," "Me," "Grumpy," and "Stinky." Christine adds: "You and your wife are in the circus audience enjoying the show."

Session 11

Christine makes another circus World. She says, "The animals are wild but they won't bite because they have been trained not to. So you could take them home with you if you wanted to."

Session 15

A World is made in which the horses are free and the coyote is trapped. Christine says of the horse (which is the white horse from her first World), "That's me!"

Subsequent sessions showed similar, relatively conflict-free scenes in which animals and people were "able to make friends." Also there is a more spontaneous verbal relationship with me.

ANALYSIS OF THE PLAY SESSIONS

In this young girl's play, we are initially shown a precursor of the play themes that will emerge later. In the first session four scenes were made. In the first scene Christine's sense of pre- occupation with a relation between the two objects is shown, and one of the objects is half alive and half dead. There is a barrenness and emptiness to the scene, allowing us to infer a severe degree of ego constriction or of actual deprivation of ego-building experi- ences. The second World has a static, lifeless quality, except per- haps for the trapped horse in the derelict castle who is (much later) identified as Christine's sense of herself.

The third scene in this first session elaborates on her pre- occupation. The motif chosen for the mother of the cub (a saber-toothed tiger) has obvious primitive and ambivalent connotations. But the tiger is not only wild, it is also searching for its lost cub, showing concern and protectiveness. The cavemen show Christine's sense of the primitive aggressive aspects of herself that are in battle with the introjects of her own mothering. The fourth scene and game reflect Christine's intuitive sense that the search for her lost aspects will involve both of us in an alternating and reciprocal arrangement. This comprehensive statement by the child on the course of her therapy has few conscious aspects. Rather, the child is showing the dominating mental images that include both her conflicted object relationships and her wish to be relieved of her domination by them.

Subsequent scenes become more complex in their interpretation, and I will retrospectively assign my own understandings to the scenes, although it should be understood that these are based on the benefits of hindsight. The line of animals in session 2 seemed to me to represent a historical construction of her own development, with tamer, "cuddly" parts at one end of the continuum and her wilder parts at the other. I felt this was an attempt to organize the various aspects of her own disposition (loving, aggressive, and so on) in some coherent way.

In the next scene from session 3 attempts are made to synthesize and bring together several aspects of Christine's inner world and the outer world of "reality." The cars at the filling station seem to me reminiscent of oral themes, such as water in a well or the feeding themes seen in Jennifer's stories. There is still, however, a stiff and almost awkward sense of stasis to the scene.

Only in the complex scene in session 4 do we begin to see movement and an "opening" of the scene in a more free but still organized fashion. A new threat has emerged. The linear organization of the train of animals has been changed so that the lions are next to the bunny and the chick. The cannons, with their explosive potential, echo the danger. The witch further shows Christine's sense of imminent doom. The previous, constricted scenes were without this danger.

We can think of this type of constriction as being one effort to minimize a perceived danger that any loosening of the personality organization would exacerbate. It might be fair to say that compulsive mechanisms in general serve to block painful or conflicted situations from entering consciousness. We can assume the continuity of unconscious theme in the sequence from the sand play to the painting. The painting shows a locked-up, "real" heart or self surrounded by many substitute hearts, a swarm of "false selves."

The scenes then begin to have a "civilized" component (shown in the contemporary buildings, cars, and so on). We can see these "civilized" scenes from session 5 onward in either of two complementary lights. The scenes could represent Christine's sense of having had two homes and two sets of parents (in particular, two mothers) who were (realistically) in conflict with one another. Or we could read these pictures as a statement about internal reality, which echoes but adds to the external situation.

In the first of these "civilized" scenes (session 5), we see that neither house can use its boat, car, or plane because the route to the outside is blocked. There is a suggestion that the enjoyment of recreation on the lake and the gasoline at the station are available somewhere, but the access to them is denied.

This seems to reflect an object world in which some aspects of the self are known or sensed to be present but are unavailable in the service of the child's problem-solving and sublimatory mechanisms because of some massive blockage. This motif echoes that of the previous scene in session 4 in which the train's progress was completely blocked by the crossing as well as being mysteriously threatened by the witch. Christine is thus demonstrating in her play her fearful fantasies, and more than that, she is drawing a map of her strengths and weaknesses, her inhibitions and libidinal blocks.

We can begin to see aspects of her broader personality: the impoverished aspects; the traumatized, primitive aspects; and the ambivalent, "which home is mine?" aspects of her more mature self. In particular, in the scene in session 5 we can take the blocked road to show Christine's sense of her own dammed-up aggression or her outwardly directed libidinal and aggressive drives. These drives have been traumatically frustrated at some point, perhaps when she was taken from her natural mother or, more probably in my view, when she was physically and repeatedly abused while in her mother's care.

In the scene in session 7 a picture is given not only of the coexistence of the two "homes"—the two aspects of her own inner reality that are revived in the transference relationship with me—but also there is the idea of a death-threatening, seemingly alien intruder. I tend to think of this as Christine's demonstration of the persecutory and dangerous aspects of her own *current* fantasy life, which undoubtedly echoes the actual abuse she had suffered as a small baby. The persecutory introject led Christine to be both cruel and vengeful to her stepmother and sister and to attack herself in fits of self-recrimination and even suicidal rage. The emergence of the coyote thus seems a turning point in Christine's attempt to come to terms with and to master this attacking aspect of her inner world.

In the *recruitment* of strengths in the scene (dogs from both houses drive off the invader), a particular process emerges. Christine realizes that she can take from other aspects of herself, or (as these are represented in the transference) that she can borrow aspects of my personality resources, to fend off the attacks she suffers in her own fantasy world. That is, a transitional mechanism has been invoked to allow aspects of Christine (or aspects of Christine-and-me) to work together to neutralize persecutory introjects.

It is this recruitment, reflecting as it does a reopening of internal channels between aspects of the personality, that allows for a sudden increase in the diversity and adaptability of the child's personality mechanisms. That is to say, it is not so much that an internalization that *replaces* the original introjects has occurred; rather, a transitional internalization of *bridging* attributes has occurred, and this allows existing aspects of the personality to work more effectively in regulating internal equilibrium.

The circus and the subsequent themes will be seen to reflect the idea that the savage animals have been tamed; the primitive aspects of Christine's character have come under ego direction and control. They may still be "wild," but they are no longer dangerous or out of control.

In Christine's case in particular, the replacement of one "home" situation and of the mother at the same time created a conflict but also laid the foundations for this rather rapid therapeutic resolution. The excellent care she had received from her stepmother had resulted in the internalization of many strengths that were readily used when Christine was able, through her treatment, to connect them to the traumatized aspects of her primitive, wounded self.

8
Reparative Change

In both of these protocols early developmental traumata that have contributed to both fixation and constriction in the personality of the child are reflected in the play themes. The reflection is not direct, of course, but rather is mediated by the intervening influence of the child's idiosyncratic style of internalization. The play acts as a holographic sampling of personality processes.

REFLECTIONS OF DEVELOPMENT IN THE PLAY THEMES

In Jennifer's case, for example, the complex motifs of hunger, greed, and destructive aggression reflect her own painful experience of disturbed feeding (she had severe abdominal pain from her colic). The co-experience of the painful aspects of the feeding and the pleasure of the suckling led to a problematic admixture of pleasure and pain or, in libidinal terms, of love and hate. This was mirrored in her mother's early intuitive idea that she was being "eaten up" and in her later, profoundly mixed feelings toward Jennifer in her differing mood states.

I do not want to cite the colic as the only determinant in this child's fixation, but I do feel that the prolonged pain associated with feeding that Jennifer suffered had a marked impact on her personality development. It is possible that the change in principal parenting from mother to father when Jennifer was 4 months old led both to (a) the oral-aggressive constellation of crystallized, primitive fantasies, and (b) the sense of sexual bivalence shown in the Lollipop Twins and in Harry Hublick's metamorphosis to Harolyn Hopeless.

121

THE CONFLUENCE OF DANGER AND LOVE

In Christine's case the situation is more difficult to decode because of the more limited developmental information. We can see much evidence of splitting and of the child's sense of imminent danger from primitive fantasies (the witch, the saber-toothed tiger, the coyote). These fantasies all show a sense of danger, yet there is a simultaneous leitmotif of care and love (e.g., the rescuing of the baby cub and its reunion with its mother). This is later amplified in the cooperative effort between the two houses to drive away the dangerous intruder.

What we can say from the history that is available and from the symptomatology when Christine was 7 (the suicidal thinking, mood extremes, and attacks on her sister and stepmother) is that there is a profound disturbance in the modulation and direction of aggression. This leaves Christine dominated by outwardly hostile or by self-punitive introjects. There is an associated failure of sublimation of aggression into cognitive or other more "advanced" mechanisms, including the mechanism of reparation. The reparative mechanism is thus shown to be deficient and needy of the investment of (a) restitutive concern, and (b) redirected persecutory hate.

We could almost speak of "reparative rage" to describe the intensity of investment the mechanism needs to be effective. But this phrase cannot be taken at its face value. The "rage" component is transformed by its ego-syntonic incorporation into the reparative process.

INFERENCES VIS-À-VIS REPARATION

In view of the relative ease with which this reparative process emerges in these and in other children, I have come to think of it as a normal, developmental mechanism whose function, formerly inhibited by traumatic vicissitudes of development, becomes released during play therapy. This function serves the purposes of reparation as Klein described them, but also acts to bolster the child's weak and as yet immature ego from daily challenges—either in the realms of reality or in those of fantasy.

THE CHANGES IN THE PLAY THEMES

In the therapeutic themes I have illustrated, morbid aspects of the child's development are articulated through play. The child's play expresses the theme in its fullest extent, as if to be sure that the savage intensity of the inner conflict is shown through the play. The emotional side of the child's play expresses need, deprivation, conflict, and suffering. The therapist's experiences with the child are therefore dual. They include (a) identification aspects of co-suffering and (b) therapeutic hopefulness and confidence in one's therapeutic technique. The second of these might all but disappear particularly with less experienced therapists and with more severely disturbed children who have especially powerful, needy ("antilibidinal") parts to their personalities.

There comes a point in the course of treatment when nascent reparative themes, present as mere hints in the early sessions, appear in a fully developed form. These themes crystallize into what I have called the reparative motif. In Christine's and in Jennifer's play it will be seen that the reparative motif initiates the phase of benign play themes and marks an end to the phase during which the child's play is dominated by conflict-ridden themes. It occurs in a way that suggests the shifting of a libidinal balance from one side to another.

HELP FROM AN OTHER

The reparative motif shows aspects of the *use of an other* in the service of solving the conflicts manifested in the play. In Jennifer's play, for example, passerby Scaley Raley helped find the food Druple Purple needed so desperately (see session 16). Christine recruited the dogs of both houses to drive off the intruding carnivore (see session 7). In the first example, Jennifer's cooperative, problem-solving story is immediately followed by a story in which the threatened figure *singlehandedly* vanquishes the threatening "scaley orange demon monster" who is "never to be seen again" (see session 17). This shows an important feature of the reparative motif; namely, that in and of itself it has an evolving character-giving, progressive autonomy to the child in the face of new conflicts. The "borrowed" strength gives way to a sense of personal autonomy and mastery over threats.

This process is analogous to the therapeutic process as a whole, in which the therapist enters the child's life for a short time and leaves the child to function with independent strengths afterward. There are clear ways in which the child does not allow the therapist to be "the solution" or even the bearer of the solution to the child. This will be shown through a clinical vignette in the discussion of the therapist's influence in Chapter 11.

THE REPARATIVE MOTIF
AND REPARATIVE MECHANISMS

Presently, the emergence of the reparative motif will be regarded as reflecting the internalization or the activation of existing, reparative mechanisms and creatively addressing intrapsychic problems as they arise. This is, of course, an extension of the original ideas of reparation, but it in no sense contradicts Klein's early formulations of the process of reparation in the resolution of the depressive position. This new formulation extends Klein's ideas of reparation in the primary love relationship to the child's broader intrapsychic functioning.

The reparative mechanism with its important role in the primary love relationship is also invoked in the resolution of conflicted situations between the child and the world, or between one aspect of the child and another. This resolution can occur in play, in daydreams, and in night dreams. The mechanism can fail to develop, or it can collapse (perhaps through being overwhelmed), or it can falter in the face of a new and particularly challenging situation (such as the birth of a sibling, the start of school, or the illness or death of a parent).

The immature psyche (to use a loose, generic term) appears to defend itself against alien ideas or dangerous percepts through the creation of a restitutive complex that neutralizes the original disturbing fantasy. The parallel with the somatic immune system's mechanism for the surrounding and neutralizing of dangerous environmental pathogens can usefully be drawn. The somatic immune system also has limitations. Some viruses proliferate more rapidly than the antibodies can be created, leading to illness; also, the somatic immune system fails to recognize certain dangerous conditions (e.g., cancer) because the illness closely simulates normal somatic processes.

This analogy should not be taken too far. But we can imagine that a beginning failure of the reparative process would lead to an accumulation of conflicted residue from the day's activities, which would in turn demand reparative processing. It might be appropriate to think of a preempting of the reparative mechanism by highly "interesting" or dominating conflicts or traumata. This would again leave the child vulnerable to collapse in a variety of "simple" tasks, such as ordinary self-direction, balanced relationships, the task of learning, the thirst for knowledge, and so forth.

THE PREOCCUPATION OF THE
CHILD BY A CONFLICT

These "dominating" conflicts, which can occupy the reparative mechanism and prevent it from its usual operations, need not be especially complex, although they are usually calamitous. A parallel in mathematics suggests itself. Logical attempts to derive a value for transcendental numbers, such as π (the ratio of the circumference to the radius of a circle), are fraught with similar peril since such numbers have no finite resolution. Early computers, asked to derive a value for π, would dedicate more and more of their computing capacity to the problem until the whole computer was occupied with this one problem.

By analogy, the child's interest and emotional energy can be preoccupied with a particular idea, "conflict," or "complex" to the exclusion of ordinary awareness of daily events and contingencies. For example, it is hard to enjoy, or even attend to, a walk in beautiful countryside if one has a stone in one's shoe (an extero-somatic irritant) or less still if one sprains one's ankle (an endo-somatic irritant). No amount of parental encouragement, discipline, self-restraint, or self-expression can correct a mental image which is coming from some fantasy production in the mind of the child.

The parents themselves may become confused in the child's mind with fantasies of dangerous monsters, and the child will then react to them with fear, or anger, or withdrawal. Teachers report similar reactions to themselves. I am assuming in these examples that the parents or the teachers are reasonably benign individuals, although subject to the vicissitudes of mood that befall most adults.

An Allegorical Illustration

The fairy tale of the Princess and the Pea offers a useful allegorical illustration at this point. I will summarize this well-known tale.

Once upon a time, in a faraway land, the King was very sad. His only daughter, a beautiful child, had been stolen soon after birth. Many years later it became time for her to assume her throne. The King sent out word for the Princess, wherever she might be, to return to the palace.

Of course, many hopeful "princesses" arrived to claim the throne and no amount of questioning could determine who was the real heiress to it.

One advisor suggested the following test: Have all the "princesses" sleep on a bed with 20 mattresses on it. Under all the mattresses would be hidden a pea. Only the real Princess would be able to tell there was a pea under the mattress because, being of royal blood, her skin would be very, very sensitive. No one else would be able to sense the presence of the pea.

The real Princess did not sleep at all during that night, and one could say from external observation that there was no reason for her not to sleep. Everyone else slept perfectly on the 20 mattresses; why was she complaining of discomfort? In real life, the Princess might even be offered a sleeping medication to relieve her distress in what she experienced as a distressing situation.

This story captures the idea of invisible problems within a child who is complaining, or withdrawing, or manifesting some signs of distress for no reason that we can see. It is certainly possible to regulate the child to conceal the distress, or at any rate to keep quiet about it. But there may remain in the child some type of focal disturbance that is manifested in a disturbance in the child's relationship to the ordinary ("real") world.

In particular, these disturbances in the child's inner world reflect themselves in emotional ways in the outside world, namely, as imbalances in the child's external object relationships. Earlier I alluded to the simple idea that internal and external relationships could be described in terms of the balance between love, hate, and reparative influences. Very much oversimplified, pictorial illustrations of a theoretical mental topography were given (see Chapter 2), but in fact these illustrations should have great complexity and also great coherence and symmetry. The molecular geneticists have provided one such complex illustration in their conceptualization of the nucleic acids (DNA, RNA) and other complex molecules (e.g., see Figure 25).

THE DISTORTING EFFECTS OF DEVELOPMENTAL VICISSITUDES

In the case illustrations presented, the "peas under the mattresses" are discernible on reflection. In Jennifer's case, a medical vicissitude—the pain of colic that prevented her from feeling well fed—was the "pea." In Christine's case, her imbalance was probably sown by the sudden discontinuity in her maternal care and the excessive mistreatment she received from her mother's boyfriend.

These early events led to distortions in the character structure of these children. By analogy with the DNA model, the events

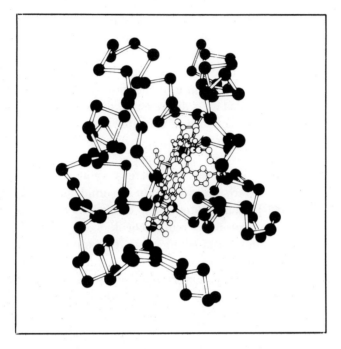

Figure 25. A molecular analog of a complex arrangement of objects in the personality (cf. Figure 7, Chapter 2). (Copyright © W. H. Freeman & Co. Reprinted by permission.)

acted as foreign bases in the structure that confuse or distort the genetic message. Similarly, these events distort the unfolding line of the developmental sequence.

In some children these same events might have acted, like a grain of sand in an oyster, as the nucleus for the development of unusual and creative diversity in the personality constellation. Every accident has its creative possibilities. On the whole, however, I think it is reasonable to believe that these severe experiences would tend toward impoverishment and limitation in the richness of the child's personality.

A child's natural play acts as a spontaneous extractor of these distorting, traumatic events. The cuddly toy, for example, allows the child to be freer to let the mother go and to play "alone" (with the cuddly toy as a reassuring companion). Play releases trapped conflicts and thus acts as if to remove the pea hidden under the mattresses in the fairy tale.

In some children (such as Jennifer and Christine), however, the residue of daily vicissitudes acts to further inhibit an already preoccupied play mechanism. Although the child may be able to play normally to some extent, some aspects of the personality may be insulated ("split off") from the play's cathartic effect. In other words, for some children the vicissitudes of life may interfere with the spontaneously reparative aspects of the personality, thus preventing a natural balance of good and bad feelings in the child. This failure of the child's ability to recover from day-to-day insults has been compared with the immune system's occasional failure to protect the child from environmental pathogens. As with the body's immune system, the weakness in the child's psychological reparative mechanism may not become apparent unless or until a challenge comes along—a specific challenge that highlights the particular immune deficiency.

These theoretical formulations of the mechanism of the recovery through play therapy lead us to a more specific consideration of the role of the therapist in promoting the child's recovery, through the recruitment and activation of reparative mechanisms. In Chapter 11, on the therapist's role in promoting the reparative mechanism's recovery and reinstatement, I will discuss similarities with the physician's options for treating failure of the body's immune response in physical illness. These options include (a) vaccination (progressive stimulation of the immune response); (b) regressive solutions (rest, being taken care of, hospitalization); (c) immune enhancement techniques (e.g., in the treatment of bone cancer using transfer factor); and (d) antibiotic administration. I will also consider the theoretical implications for personality development that are illuminated by the discovery of the reparative motif.

9
Reparation
in Therapy with
an Adult

The possibility that the reparative motif is a central manifestation of recovery in all psychotherapy is an attractive proposition. I now offer a detailed illustration of the emergence and confluence of themes in the work I did some time ago with a young adult woman. This work shows something of my approach to psychotherapy, in which I try to limit my interventions to what the patient herself has already introduced as a theme. This has the result, in the case I present, of delaying any mention of this young woman's parents for many months. I avoid questioning about life's details in "reality," preferring to permit the course of associations to find its own way to express necessary themes. I have elaborated other aspects of my approach during the unfolding of this story now and in the next chapter, in which I consider my subjective experience of the psychotherapy situation.

This adult case shows the reflection of pathognomonic themes in the verbal associations of a young woman being seen in psychotherapy in a hospital clinic. In spite of the grayness of the setting, the atmosphere of the sessions was charged and sometimes colorful. The themes show the linkage between mistrust, the sense of having been poisoned (see Klein's ideas on the poisoned breast, an extreme form of the fantasy of the bad, absent, or depriving breast), and the distortion in this young woman's view of herself as a recipient and giver of love. She saw herself damaged as a love partner and as a potential mother. After many months of treatment the mutative links to her own mother's illness became accessible, and with accessibility, release from their domination occurred. However, I must emphasize that I saw this as the final step in a long building process rather than as a discontinuity when health suddenly supervened. A unique and moving feature of this young woman's treatment was her use of a doll, preserved from childhood, to speak for her; through it she was able to express ideas more freely than had she been talking about her own thoughts. This reflects a child's use of symbol and miniature as the medium for communication about difficult or painful aspects in the child's experience.

The doll, Muffie*, had been the young woman's constant companion since childhood and through college. Unlike my description of a transitional object as something that acts as a bridge between a mother in her presence and a mother in her absence, this doll appeared to have served the young woman as a buffer between herself and her very disturbed mother.

Reparative themes in adult psychotherapy are contained in sometimes subtle thematic changes. I have regarded the "free associations" of the adult as equivalent to the fantasy productions or the dreams of a child: a part of the golden road to the unconscious. In spite of the "real" significance of the themes, my understanding and interpretations are predicated on the assumption that the patient has deeper levels of the mind, which are being both revealed and hidden by the sophistication of adult language.

I have included my discussion of this case concurrently with the case material to allow the reader to follow more readily my own train of inferential reasoning, obscure as it may still appear at times. The case is chosen specifically to illustrate emergence of the reparative motif, but it is nevertheless not untypical of adult recovery in psychotherapy in my experience. It is a hackneyed axiom that Jungian analysts' clients have archetypal dreams, Freudians' clients have oedipal dreams, and Kleinians' clients have Kleinian dreams. The process also applies to verbal associations, from the first minutes of the first hour of work together. I ask the reader to bear this phenomenon in mind during the description of this young woman's treatment.

Diane was a 22-year-old graduate student in a department of

---

*Various names and details have been changed to protect the identity of the young woman, whose contribution to this work I gratefully acknowledge.

physiology at a private medical college in an Eastern state. She was seen once a week for six months, a duration determined by the academic timetable.

Session 1

There were long silences in this session, and there was little eye contact between Diane and myself. She seemed most at ease when I looked out of the window. Diane said that she had sought a place at the student dormitory and was given not one but two reasons she could not stay. She concluded that the authorities were deliberately denying her a place.

Later in the hour she recounted her difficulties in an apartment house where she used to live: the proprietor had asked her to put out the garbage. Diane had left rather than do this. Her present landlady served moldy or maggot-ridden food; hence the urgency of finding a place in the dormitories.

Here we see two related themes: the first relates to the function of the world, the mother, the analyst, as a container welcoming the individual and *making room for* her. In this respect, we see the idea that the person must have emotional room, independence, security in order to feel safe. This idea is juxtaposed with the theme of bad food and garbage: we can think both of an untrusted breast providing nurturance contaminated with (for example) anxiety, guilt, or rage, and of the idea of the *parent's* duty to "put out the garbage" —to render the home clean and (emotionally) healthy. My analysis of the theme as I had noted it at the time was "an attempt to separate from dirt and filth that Diane is afraid she may incorporate." If I had thought further, I could perhaps have understood that the fear was of incorporating "filth" from me during the treatment.

Session 2

Diane began by saying that she had food poisoning. She noticed the sink in my consulting room with some relief and said she might have to use it.

She described the advances made to her by another student, which she had tried to discourage, but he is "much stronger than I." She had written to him to say that he should stop treating her as a piece of feminine flesh and that either she would have to find a way to control him or avoid him.

My consulting room already had become a place to vomit poisoned food, to get rid of it. I was to absorb Diane's unwanted bad feelings. The associated fear of me as a man implicitly dangerous is introduced.

Session 3

Diane spoke first about moving away from the moldy food to a new place. She said, ostensibly about the moving: "If I keep on avoiding what I am looking for, there will be nothing left." The theme moved on to her lover and her fears of him. I asked if I could hear "more about fearing people," which initiated a fifteen-minute silence that I did not interrupt. Eventually Diane said: "In situations, if I do not do as others do, or as they expect of me, they might, and have, acted against me." I replied: "What might I expect of you?" trying to put her worry about me into words.

In the first theme there is a hopeful sign, that perhaps there exists a place where the food is not moldy. On the other hand, reflecting what I now see as a broad fear of love, is the statement about avoiding "what I am looking for." Here we see the essence of an intrapsychic conflict. The awareness that one wants and is looking for something (love, security, a sexual relationship) is simultaneously experienced with the awareness that one is avoiding that very thing.

Part of the reason for this contradiction, this "split," is announced in the idea that one has to watch out for other people acting against one. This thought is not a simple one. People act "against" one another in any relationship whenever they disagree or even differ in their views. As I indicated earlier, the interpolation of love and aggression in the mind and in relationships is a central dilemma. The question in Diane's mind at this early point seemed to be how safe she would be to depend on me in the face of my possibly "acting against" her, whatever this might mean to her.

Session 4

The first topic was "I am moving tomorrow." Diane had found a new apartment. Also Diane mentioned her childhood doll, Muffie, which she said she would bring the next time. The doll does not like mirrors.

The baby's first mirror is the mother's face reflecting to the baby the baby's own mood. After mentioning the move "tomorrow" to a new home, Diane says that on our "morrow" she will begin her emotional move with the help of her doll. She has found a language she can use.

Session 5

Diane brought along a brown paper bag in which she had the rag doll, Muffie. "Although she looks harmless, the end of her hair has stingers, and these stingers contain Muffie venom. Although it is not visible, Muffie has a long forked tongue and is related in this way to snakes. Through the venom, she is related to toadstools and mushrooms. At home Muffie sits next to a vase and lures people in order to sting them. She would like to hatch a Muffie egg, but she is not sure if there can ever be such a thing. She has looked around for a suitable egg and has concluded that she will have to lay one in order to have the pleasure of hatching one."

Here the poisonous other has become a poisonous self. Muffie is related to snakes, vases, and egg-laying. She is capable of both poisoning and egg-hatching.

The complex relation of the internal sense of self and the view of relationships with others begins to be seen here. It is not at all clear that the self/not-self distinction can be made. Projective identification, the seeing in others aspects of oneself, confuses who is who.

Session 6

"For some years Muffie was in hibernation, like a vegetable. When she came out of this, she stung my father first, then my brother. When she has a bath, all her insides are taken out and replaced with new kapok."

Here is a possible symbolic solution to the problem of feeling full of poison: to take out one's insides each bath time and replace them. The repertoire of Muffie's actions so far is quite limited. We know she stings and hibernates.

(The seventh session was cancelled by my secretary as I had a cold.)

Session 8

"Muffie is green inside. No one can see this. She avoids vertical straight lines and long thin objects. There is such a lot of pollution these days. There are so many smokestacks and so many people: when smokestacks and people get too close they become offensive.

Smokestacks cause pollution which, if you cannot control, you have to avoid."

I remarked that this phrase was the same one Diane had used about her boyfriend in her letter to him.

"When fields are cultivated, people spoil the soil, the virgin earth. Pollution has already occurred. It is too late to avoid it. I just have to control it in the future."

Here is a combination of two themes, showing the condensation of two emotional conflicts into one. The sense of having been poisoned, suffocated by too much closeness, is combined with the sexual motif of long thin objects, smokestacks that pollute, and things that take away virginity. We see here the way in which early nurturance (oral) themes are added to the perception of sexual relations. The notion of love contained here is one of suffocation, and worse, of poisoning.

Session 9

"Muffie is not here today. She is bored when she is here and we do not talk about her. It has been a frustrating week at work. The technicians are off sick or not around when you want them."

"The trouble is that we are overcrowded at work. Overcrowding gets things damaged."

I intervened at this point to repeat the phrase from the last session: "like chimneys and people which are offensive if they get too close."

Diane replied: "They take away my clean flasks if I leave them about. Things get *broken* due to overcrowding. It is like putting wet things (glassware) into a hot oven: it is quicker but more dangerous that way."

Diane went on to describe her plans to visit her parents at Christmas. "They are getting old. They must need their children more as they get older."

This hour commenced with an obvious allusion to my having been absent and ill: unavailable when needed. The repetitive allusions to overcrowding causing damage are perhaps reflections of Diane's sense of the dangers of depending on someone. In particular, they may disappear ("be ill") when you most need them. The seemingly simple reference to my illness contains what would prove to be a most important theme: the testing of my reaction to the statement of what a "frustration" my illness is. In fact, Diane's mother has suffered from repeated "illnesses" (actually psychotic collapses) throughout Diane's life. Her reference to her parents needing her more is perhaps both realistically true and a reflection of Diane's own childhood sense of desperate need for a stable love object. In the absence of such an object the available objects take on a persecutory "flavor" or at worst, are felt to be poisonous. I thought the "wet things into hot oven" theme obviously had to do with coitus, but I could not elaborate the relevance of the theme.

What was broken, according to the next session's themes, was the sense of being oneself, of being a person.

Session 10

"Muffie is not feeling herself today. She had too much to drink last night at a party." The theme continued with Diane stating her need to be in control of situations, relationships. I made the mistake of asking a transference-related question: to what extent did she feel she had to control me? Diane replied that while I might get crazy ideas about her, that was all right with her so long as I did not act on them. She added, in a tone of chilling seriousness, "Others have, on occasion, acted against me."

We see two themes again intertwined: the sense of loss of "feeling yourself" and the loss of control. In an emotionally chaotic atmosphere, keeping control may be the only way to retain a sense of who you are. This is nevertheless too much to ask of a small child.

Session 11 (First session after the vacation.)

Diane was 20 minutes late to the session. She was very wet, having come through a rainstorm with no protection. Her sense of having been hurt extended to a neglect of her own comfort. She talked about her mother "having trouble with her eyes. She is afraid she will have to see the eye doctor again. She has no faith in eye doctors," Diane added, "and neither have I."

Let me interpolate my conjecture, derived with hindsight, that Diane was speaking of an "I" doctor, someone who treats the sense of who you are, who "I" represents.

Diane had also had trouble with "eye doctors." She had been given atropine drops for a week, which made it impossible for her to focus, to see, and then was told that nothing needed to be done.

She feels that the prospect of "drops in the eye" is equivalent to danger, to pollution. She added, in a sudden change of emotional tone from suspiciousness to candor, something even approaching trust, that she feels "safer coming to see you than going to see an eye doctor, because if you say something which I criticize, I know you will not be dogmatic. You will not put drops in my eye against my will."

To judge by the shift in the emotional tone at this point in the session, there was a reparative component in this motif. If we take the theme "drops in the eye" to mean (a) drops in the "I"—collapses in the sense of self, (b) intrusions into her ability to see, dogmatic assertions that render Diane "unable to focus," and (c) polluting drops of semen in her womb, then we see the importance of the added condition "against my will." This person's sense of the effectiveness of her own will had been so eroded as to leave her feeling almost helpless, at the mercy of the world. The sense of ego-syntonic aggression, used to defend and advance the self in the world, also had been "broken" or at any rate seriously inhibited.

In determining the content of the associations centering on this mutative moment in the treatment, there are the historically determined aspects of Diane's personality—her vulnerability and narcissistic woundedness—but she also has chosen an aspect of me that is a prominent part of my character: my reticence and reluctance to be too insistent on my own point of view. Although I am capable of being tenacious about some things, the part of myself that this young woman might have seen most clearly is this "undogmatic" part. I mention this to adduce that reparation occurs when the patient can find in the therapist, in spite of all the therapist's impairments, a specific and desperately wanted strength. In allowing him or herself to be "read" by the patient, the therapist allows the patient to seek out these wanted aspects.

This session marked the beginning of exchanges between Diane and myself in which the pathognomonic and reparative elements of our relationship were more defined. Also, the effects of the approaching end of our brief work together began to be appreciable.

Session 12

Diane was again late, by a few minutes. She was wearing a pink blouse that struck me in contrast to the more subdued colors she usually wore. She began (literally) to let her hair down but then did not. I have only very scant notes on this session.

Session 13

Diane talked about her experiences with a psychiatrist previously (the "I" doctor?). He had suggested medication for her. I made some intervention to redirect her attention to her fears about what I would do to her, which was taken as an attack.

"You are driving me into a corner. Trying to impose restrictions on me." (Long pause.) "Because I am unwilling or unable to do something does not mean I am afraid of it. Some things need privacy."

I replied (compounding my error): "What things are you referring to?"

"You are driving me into a corner again."

"I'm trying to draw you out of of it," I said.

"Like a spider and a fly," she answered.

My error, in trying to direct the theme, resulted in a vigorous exchange in which the poison/eating/sexuality theme reemerged as a direct aspect of the therapeutic relationship. The confrontation was not over.

Session 14

"You seem to want me to talk about ____ [name of the place Diane lived]. Nowhere has ever been so favorable to me."

This theme was elaborated into how Diane was *being seen* differently by other people. Now people were commenting on how much she had changed, how she looked better. I made some comment that perhaps she too was seeing the world differently, looking at things in a more favorable light.

She replied: "If you look at people it might seem that you are staring. There are various ways of looking. There is the *penetrating* look [her emphasis]. This is uncomfortable but not threatening. Then there is the 'pleading' look used by men sometimes. Then there is the critical look my father uses on me. There is the dishonest look my former professor used. Also there is the bored, fed-up look you sometimes give me. It seems you are more interested in certain things than in others. That influences what I am going to say."

Here is a session of contrasts. On the one hand, there is the favorable description of Diane's circumstances; on the other, the very mixed views of men: critical, dishonest, pleading, bored, and so on. Perhaps this is the beginning of an integration of realistic perceptions of men's varying moods into the matrix of feeling relatively accepted and well liked. On a more primitive level, the impact of how other people view Diane on her own view of herself is being reconsidered.

Session 15

"Now I can breathe again. It is so stuffy in the waiting room." The theme moved on to a party to which Diane had gone the previous night. Speaking of the men there, she said disconsolately, "They seemed like monsters, all monsters." I repeated in an unquestioning way: "All monsters." Diane corrected me: "Not everyone is a monster. Most people I have nothing to do with at all."

There is a return to the earlier theme of suffocation perhaps by the monster-men at the party, too numerous, too close, too polluting. In the face of this world-view, Diane withdraws into herself. (Muffie, the doll, was brought into the room each time and was seated next to Diane. Muffie's presence helps Diane to speak more directly about herself.) Are men monsters, and if so what does it mean to be a woman?

Session 16

"Last week you accused me of selecting undesirable types of men." (My statement about men as monsters, although a restatement, appeared to have meant to Diane that she must be selecting monsters from the men in the world.) "I have some letters here from someone I used to know. He thought of me as *female* [scornfully] too."

Here we see the continued struggle with what it is to be a woman, to be "female," or to be viewed as female by a man. I said that I understood being female could be a problem, especially if you were with a man who seemed like a monster.

Diane replied: "I could say you are a vertebrate and not a jellyfish but I do not think that every time I see you. I could not be sure without giving you a dissection. You would have to take all your clothes off and lie down on the dissection table" (laughter).

I had wondered whether dissection was in fact dis-sex-ion, removing the threat of me as a male. At the same time, there was a playful seductiveness in her idea of the dissection. At another level, Diane's quest may be that of taking me apart to see how men function or to see what is inside me. Do I have poison inside me or something nourishing, hate or love to offer to her? The answer followed quickly.

Session 17

"I have been poisoned." (Long silence.) I eventually asked, "Who poisoned you?" Diane replied that the fume cupboards at work had been blowing out instead of sucking in.

"Either I have to avoid them altogether or we need a new fume cupboard. The trouble is that people do not take precautions until it is too late. What I really need is an internal gas mask. The trouble is they are not too easy to get hold of."

I had mixed associations to these themes. The question of how to avoid poisoning is at so many levels that I thought of at least two: Can one avoid being poisoned by men or people in general if they are too close? Is closeness itself a poison? And linked to the physiology laboratory theme, can one avoid being poisoned (impregnated?) by a man in a sexual encounter? However, a startling link is now made between the poison theme and Diane's relationship with her mother.

Session 18

"I had a letter from my mother. She is having eye trouble again. She has said it's me—my chemicals are damaging her eyes *by their fumes*" [my emphasis]. I called her—she is a dreadful creature and I told her so. . . . Have you heard of Professor _____? He is in the biology department, where I was looking for a job. He invited me to go to see him. He was very good to me [weeping]. But I still could not get support from the National Institutes of Health to work with him. I almost gave up and became a hermit."

The chemicals theme returns as the damaging agent between Diane and her mother. The reference to a man is now a benign one, an inviting one. But he is forbidden by an outside agency, perhaps the unsupportive mother. Here is Diane's sense of her own poisonousness, her own danger, which necessitates that she become a hermit. The danger can be removed only if she sees herself as distinctively different from her mother.

(Session 19 has been omitted from this discussion.)

Session 20

"I have applied for a job as a dorm counselor. The chair of my department wrote me a reference. He said how much I had changed. How I used to be very shy and now everyone in the department likes me. He says, generalizing from the particular, that I must get along well with people. I used to put people off when I was at interviews."

I asked if she felt she was putting me off in some way. She replied, "Heavens no. The worst I have ever done here was to call you a spider."

"In some species, the female spider eats the male," I noted. "Are you saying I am attacking you?" she asked.

"Not exactly. I was meaning eating me, consuming me the way people do . . . take one another inside as it were."

Diane interrupted to ask what I meant by consuming; I asked what she had understood by what I said. She answered: "That is like two people breaking bits off one another or getting so stuck they cannot ever separate. Or being swallowed whole, disintegrating."

I replied that I thought perhaps Diane's ideas about love were as consumptive, disintegrative, damaging.

Session 21

"I talked to my mother again. She is complaining of having floating bodies in her eyes. I think she is very upset since my brother and I left home."

"You and he are her 'floating bodies'?"

"She blamed us for ruining her eyesight and then leaving."

"Your leaving your mother might have distressed her."

"There are some things, like leaving, that you just have to do even though they are distressing."

"I will have to leave you soon," she added. "Last week I thought I had your aroma but I have not chewed you up yet. Or shall I swallow you whole, like an oyster?"

I said, "When you came, you were talking about bad food. The question might be, if you eat and chew me up, will I be a good oyster or a bad one? Will I be good to eat or poisonous?"

Diane talked about her fears about going to visit her parents in the imminent holiday (the spring break).

Two themes again are concurrently visible: the necessity of separation, of individuation, even if it distresses the other, and the theme of reparative introjection, taking inside a sense of value rather than one of poison.

Session 22 (After a three-week break.)

Diane began speaking fast and agitatedly with none of the usual pauses. I felt she was "not allowing me into the room."

"My mother is in a dreadful state." Diane described her mother's symptoms: feelings of persecution, a preoccupation with cleaning the toilet, talking continuously about her distress. I interrupted to say, "That must have been terrible for you." She cried a little and said that the worst of it was to be held responsible for her mother's condition, even by her father. She said that her mother and her mother's sister both had these tendencies. There used to be another sister. "She's dead. She took an overdose of tranquilizers."

I will pause in my description of the clinical material here to give some observations about the course of unfolding material. Early in the treatment Diane's concerns were about her own inner sense of badness and the danger she perceived from others, especially men, when she came close to them. As the inner balance changed in her perception of herself, and others began to see her in a favorable light, Diane was able to describe from her own perspective her mother's condition, having somewhat distanced herself from processes involving herself and her mother (indentification, internalization, the narcissistic image derived from the mother, and so on). Her own regression around the visit to her parents' home was short-lived. I soon felt that she had regained her composure and hope.

Some of this recovery is based on her idealization of me, some on her realistic perceptions of my personal style, some on technical interventions I had made. It may be said that in adult treatment, the successor to the reparative moment is a differentiation of the self from introjected sources of "badness," particularly those with infantile origins. In treatment as brief as I have described, the question of temporary remission or of transference cure are both relevant. I am using this case illustration without addressing that issue. My concern here is to elucidate selective themes that seem to herald the activation of inner reparative mechanisms based on any available mechanism or set of mechanisms that the individual can recruit.

Diane continued to describe herself and her mother in contrasting terms, striving, as it were, for greater differentiation.

(Session 23 will not be discussed here.)

Session 24

Diane arrived early, by bicycle. For the first time she took off her coat. She recollected calling me an oyster and said that, to go by my aroma, I must be a good oyster. On the other hand, "My father is like a limpet. Very stubborn and obstinate. My mother has been threatened with ECT [electroconvulsive therapy] if she does not recover in a couple of weeks taking medication. I am not keen on everyone taking medication. If they do, the world will become so bad that all the sensitive people will have to take pills to bear it."

Later in the hour she spoke of "being on equal terms with the professors at a conference," which I took as a reflection of her feeling more equal with me, less having to idealize me. There is also a hint of sympathy for her ill mother, a "sensitive" person.

Session 25

"Muffie has only her nightdress on today. She apologizes. She was up very late last night. I have become more like Muffie, more dragonlike, that is, more assertive. My father cannot dominate me any more. He is like a lizard. The sort who destroys. He might destroy my seed bed with his mechanical cultivator."

"Men with mechanical cultivators can be very dangerous," I commented.

"Yes, they can corrupt . . . pollute."

Diane editorialized at this point: "Why do we always speak about things in such devious ways?"

I reflected on the question and asked, "Why indeed?"

"I have to have some protection, especially outside here. So I speak in this way. Not everybody can understand me."

(Session 26 is omitted from discussion here.)

Session 27

Muffie is holding a dandelion flower and is set carefully on the chair next to Diane. "My mother is having delusions about her appearance. She thinks the drugs are damaging her mind. She feels everyone is plotting against her. Irrespective of how much or little I contributed to her condition in the past, I should see that she is treated properly now."

Here is a new reparative theme addressed ostensibly to the mother but in fact relating to Diane's sense of taking care to see that she herself is "treated properly." She has developed new relationships with men at her work, one of them a physician, whom she described as treating her well. The restoration of inner balance makes for a different disposition, even to highly charged situations such as one's mother in a psychotic episode.

"The doctor saw my mother for a few minutes and told her to come back in six weeks." This was also a reference to the fact that she and I have only six weeks left to the end of the academic year and of her work with me. This factor may have put additional pressure on Diane to de-idealize and decathect me, reinvesting herself in new relationships in her everyday life. The work Diane was doing to preserve me after her therapy ended became evident in the following hour.

Session 28

Muffie was carrying a little weed flower. "People should not put weed killer on rosebeds. I don't approve of it."

Here we see Diane taking a stand to assert her view of herself as a rosebed that should not have been and should not now be poisoned.

"Muffie likes to shelter under the leaves of weeds. You can find shade in the middle of a patch of parsley, so long as you take care not to get stepped on."

"Muffie keeps me company in bed. She's soft and cuddly. She watches me as I go to sleep and she is always there in the morning."

I said, "There is no danger that she will leave you," alluding to the probable sense of abandonment the end of her therapy was occasioning.

"Muffie wonders what you will do after we stop coming here. Muffie wants to do something outrageous. She wants to tell you a secret." Muffie sat on my shoulder as if to tell me a secret and stung my ear with her Muffie sting. But it might have been a kiss. The secret is that Muffie's stings are really kisses. As she was putting Muffie back into her bag, Diane said, "You'll miss Muffie" and I agreed. "I'll miss you too," I added.

Session 29

Diane was wearing a new coat, her eyes running with "hay fever." She complained on Muffie's behalf that it was no fun being locked up all week and only coming out once. She should be brought out every day. Hal, Diane's new colleague, says hello to Muffie every day.

"Muffie thinks you are very dull today. Why don't you see her every day?"

"Mother now feels my father is in league with the doctors who are poisoning her with pills."

We can only imagine the complexities intrinsic to this young woman's attempts to live with her schizophrenic mother when Diane was a baby. It may be that her mother had phases of relative health, but we can now see a new meaning in the early themes of "having no place to go" and of having been poisoned herself. The fantasy goes far beyond Klein's idea of the poisonous breast. In the real world Diane's aunt was poisoned, and her mother constantly feared being poisoned, eventually attributing the source of the poison to her daughter. Nevertheless, the Kleinian idea of penis/breast equivalence is shown in the juxtaposition of the fear of being poisoned by food and the fear of being poisoned by insemination. There is surely a further component in the poison idea: the medication given to help her mother was used by her aunt to kill herself. Perhaps here we see the problem of "poisoned love" of the profoundly ambivalently held breast, rendering future love relations terrifyingly bipolar.

Session 30

Diane arrived looking pale and wan. She said, "I have been sick on the sidewalk and I was given tea by the janitor. I will probably be sick again." She moaned and attempted to be sick in the office sink (cf. session 2) for some 20 minutes.

Here is the idea of sickness and care: the janitor, the person who cleans up, ministered to Diane after she was sick. This contrasts with her early themes of being made sick (by her landlady) with the food she was given. "Hal and I were at a party last night and he gave me too much to drink. I thought he was going to take me back to his place but he took me to my house instead [perhaps a man who does not take advantage of Diane]. When I do not feel well at work, Hal makes me a cup of coffee. Why don't you make me one?"

Some minutes later Diane said she had been wondering what she would have said to me had I been at the party the previous evening.

Here is the beginning of dyscathectic rage, getting rid of me emotionally to prepare for the imminent end of our work. The aggression, mild as it may seem, based on the limitations on my care for Diane (I did not make her tea or coffee as the janitor and Hal had), reflects what Diane felt as she sensed the limitations imposed on her mother's care by her mother's illness. The confirmation of this hypothesis came rapidly, thanks to a visit to town by her parents. However, I will allude again to the more benign aspect to her own "sickness" as it was presented in this hour.

Session 31

Diane was early. She began with "I'm on my way to put the eggs in the incubator. I have left them in the art gallery. They do not know where I am."

I had not known about the visit Diane was having from her parents so I replied: "The eggs?"

"No, my parents."

In this opening remark there is an important theme: Diane feels she can safely "incubate eggs" herself so long as her parents are safely in the local art gallery/museum—the place where relics are kept as well as beautiful *objets d'art*. The mood of the rest of the hour was again such as to leave me feeling shut out and only in the last minutes, when I had begun to be paralyzed with a sense of failure, did Diane stop her rapid talking, cry floods of tears, and somehow manage to end by smiling through her tears. My notes indicate a "muddled barrage of topics," which I was quite unable to follow or record in the notes.

Session 32

"I have got rid of the old creatures on the plane. They took the night flight back home. They argued all the time they were here; they were shouting at one another in the street." She said that while her parents were both in tears, arguing and very pessimistic, Muffie had not become so upset: she had kept hidden until they were about to leave.

Diane herself cried gently again and said she could now look at her parents and see them "circling around inside their cage."

Diane clearly saw herself as outside the cage. But what of the cage of her psychotherapy, her dependency on me? She asked, "I wonder what you will be doing afterward. Do you have a nest of your own, perhaps with little eggs in it?" She went on to speculate about my life after she stopped seeing me, which I felt contained some nuclei of her ideas for her own future. In considering the ending, Diane wept and smiled simultaneously, although it was clearly necessary for her to be quite cautious as to how much she said about our work together. In fact she brought a huge bundle of notes she had prepared for our last hour together.

Session 33

Muffie was seated next to me on my desk and Diane was looking directly at me, almost piercingly. She took out her notes and began: "First, this is our last hour," then cried for a few minutes. She went on to read that although she had changed over the year and it was a change for the better, the change brought new problems.

She went on with a vigorous train of topics, which she read in a somewhat detached way. I interrupted at some point to say that I knew this was a difficult hour for her and that I was finding it difficult too.

When it was time to end the hour, Diane burst into tears once more but was smiling through them again.

The necessary aggression that might have made the last hours less painful was masked by various factors in this case. Not only was therapy ending prematurely but there was the complicating factor of Diane's mother's illness supervening when it did, somewhat obscuring ending processes. Nevertheless, the sustained new balance of hope over pessimism can be seen in each of the last few hours of therapy.

The reader may have had difficulty in seeing in these transcripts the clarity of the reparative shift in the internal balance of the emotions. The changes were occurring at many levels of fixation simultaneously and were concealed by "devious" language. In fact, there is probably *no* language, however symbolic, that can adequately reflect the inner experience of the adult undergoing the changes that psychotherapy initiates.

It will also be evident that the treatment of Diane may have precipitated the decompensation her mother experienced. I will address this topic and the problem it creates in the treatment of children and adults in the chapter on reparation in the family constellation.

10

Beyond
Countertransference:
Activity in the Mind of
the Therapist

This chapter examines the activities in the minds of both the therapist and the patient in the course of expressive psychotherapy. The two activities will be seen to be related but not altogether consonant. The degree to which the discursive (verbal) exchange between therapist and patient reflects the mental activity of each will be discussed. The focus of the analysis will be on the light that is shed on the determinants and contents of the activity in the mind of the therapist.

Mental activity has its origins in the womb, at some indeterminate stage of embryonic development, and continues through every waking and sleeping moment of the individual's life. The contents and articulation of an adult's thoughts depend partly on the internal object relations of the individual and partly on external relationships between the individual and the "real" world. This "real" world includes other contemporary individuals, and in this chapter I will examine the phenomena in the mind of the therapist confronted by another individual, the patient. For convenience, I will arbitrarily separate my consideration of the therapist's mentation into the following categories.

1. *Conscious responses.* Conscious thoughts respondent to the patient's associations or comments. (For example, a patient says, "It's a nice day," and the therapist thinks, Yes, it is. The therapist may even verbalize these thoughts.)

2. *Countertransference—initiated thoughts.* Irrational or, at best, rationalized thoughts stimulated by more or less primitive processes in the patient—processes not only verbalized by the patient but also communicated by the patient's attitude to the therapist (e.g., the patient idealizes the therapist; the therapist basks in the experiential glow of inflated self-esteem).

3. *Autochthonous thoughts and fantasies.* Associations and thoughts generated by the therapist relatively independent of the patient or of the patient's associations. This category, *sui generis*, reflects some of the wellspring of thoughts that go on in the therapist's mind, whether or not with a patient (e.g., I'm dying for a cup of tea; I must remember to write to _____; I want to go to the shore this weekend). However, this category includes preoccupations about a particular patient experienced outside the hour; somewhat countertransferential but closer to category 3 than to 2.

These categories clearly overlap and there is a fluid exchange among them. My purpose in this division into categories is simply to organize this study, to provide a framework for comparison and discussion. I will consider them in turn.

CONSCIOUS RESPONSE

The secondary process level of interaction between therapist and patient is overt and accessible to introspection, and it follows the rules of ordinary logic. Even at this level, however, there will be a more or less complex connection between what the patient says (presumably connected with what the patient is thinking) and what the therapist says. Consider the following exchange (from Chapter 9):

Example 1.

Patient: "There are so many chimneys and so many people. When chimneys and people are too close they become offensive. Chimneys cause pollution which if you can't control you have to avoid" (from session 6).

Therapist: "I recall you said in the first time you came to see me, speaking of your boyfriend, that you had told him either you would have to find a way to control him or you would avoid him."*

In this example, the therapist, using a phrase that the patient herself has used in two different contexts, is making an associative link between the patient's feeling about polluting chimneys and her boyfriend. The therapist thus alludes, mutatis mutandis, to the patient's sense of being polluted (inseminated by her boyfriend's dangerous chimney/penis). (The material in support of this allusion is contained both in the above extract and in other material not here reported.) By referring to the assonant phrase, the therapist is using his memory to complement the therapeutic exchange, consciously and deliberately. There was a wide range of choice available to the therapist here: (a) to say nothing, (b) to encourage further associations, or (c) to intervene in some way. The intervention chosen sprang from the assonance of the phrase used by the patient to describe pollution with the same phrase used some weeks previously. The therapist did not search his memory; rather the echoed phrase sprang out demanding his attention. This level of the process, this "springing out," is not under conscious determination and falls more properly into the phenomena of category 3, which I will discuss later.

Example 2.

Patient: "What time is it? Is it time to stop?"
Therapist:
   (*a*) "There are five minutes more."
   (*b*) "You want some signal from me even though you can see the clock. What could that be about?"
   (*c*) "How much can you fit into an hour, a day, a week, a lifetime? When should you restrain yourself and say 'It's time to stop' or when to let yourself go and push on society's limits?"
   (*d*) "You're wondering what time it is and when we stop."

---

*cf. "Sisters of Mercy," The Songs of Leonard Cohen: "Yes, you who must leave everything that you cannot control, it begins with your family and soon it comes round to your soul." CBS Records, Copyright © 1966, Stranger Music. All rights reserved.

These rather contrived examples of alternative replies illustrate another, perhaps more pedestrian style of verbal therapist response. The most mechanical of such responses can assume an automaton-like stereotypy. These illustrations show simple conscious and direct connection between what the patient says and what the therapist thinks (including possible replies). It is, of course, inevitable that the therapist while saying one thing is actually thinking a whole range of other things that are not reported to the patient. Faced with the question of example 2 above, after enduring an hour with a very demanding patient, the therapist might think, Five minutes more but it seems like an eternity. Or with an especially liked patient: Five minutes more. Would that it were longer. In each case the therapist might say only, "There are five minutes more." There is, so to speak, a level of therapeutic discretion of subterfuge, at its extreme, in the response to the patient. This occurs because of the demands of prudence and therapeutic wisdom and is not disingenuous on the part of the therapist. On the contrary, the careful selection of what verbal contributions to make, even at this relatively overt level, conditions the working alliance and allows work at the other levels of therapeutic discourse. I will now turn to the second of these levels, that of countertransference.

COUNTERTRANSFERENCE

Countertransference reactions are highly idiosyncratic, and the following examples are thus very general. Consider an oral-dependent/oral-aggressive patient who is complaining about "how badly life treats me" (including how unsatisfactory the therapist seems).

> *Patient (angrily)*: "You don't help me, you just sit there while I suffer."

The therapist may feel or even respond with (a) anger that mirrors that of the patient's oral sadistic parts, (b) sympathy or grieving with the patient's "bad life," (c) reactive therapeutic zeal to overcome the therapist's and patient's sense of uselessness of the hour, or (d) passive withdrawal from the patient's attack.

The therapist uses his or her awareness of these inner responses as a heuristic guide to the patient's unconscious world and tries to respond with a level of interpretation appropriate to the patient's emotional readiness. A follower of Melanie Klein might say, "I seem to you like a bad breast, unresponsive and depriving you of the very things you need to live"; or the therapist might try to interpret the counterpart to the patient's aggressive fantasy: "You see me as bad through your terror of seeing me as good and dependable. You hate me so as not to experience the admixture of loving and hating feelings you actually hold inside you."

Interpretations belong in category 1 but are clearly derived from mental activity in the therapist at the other two levels, 2 and 3. Countertransference responses form category 2, but they too have some derivation from level 3, to which I will now turn my attention.

AUTOCHTHONOUS THOUGHTS AND FANTASIES

These incidental thoughts, seemingly peripheral in the therapist's mind and to the process of therapy itself, have nevertheless proved a valuable subject of study in their own right. During a therapeutic hour, the therapist may concentrate to a greater or lesser degree on what the patient is saying and on his or her own consequent thoughts. It has been my practice for some years to try to let my mind wander during psychotherapy, vaguely monitoring the course of my mind's meanderings as I do so. One effect of this practice on my patients has been that as I let my mind wander, I find that their associations also become freer, thus allowing the patient better spontaneous access to many hidden areas of their own personality.

The degree to which I can accomplish this task, this freeing of my own thoughts to wander, depends on the patients' dependency or on their insistence that I attend to every word they are saying. I am not fond of the style of therapeutic interaction in which patient and therapist hang on each other's every word as if their life depended on it. I would go so far as to say that I feel that shared silences in the therapeutic hour, rather than manifesting resistance, can be most important times of mental and emotional percolation for the therapist and the patient. A good deal of deep therapeutic work can occur in these silences. Balint (1958) refers to a "third area of the mind" in which creative forces are at work, and he states explicitly that in his view it is in silence that the patient communicates with this part of his or her mind. I distinguish here between a receptive and a rejecting silence. I am also very much in agreement with Mackie (1969), who emphasized the importance of serving patients according to their emotional needs for intimacy or distance.

Bergson (1912), the noted logical positivist of the early part of the twentieth century, distinguished two profoundly different forms of knowing, the first of which implies that we move around an object, the second that we enter into it. The patient's knowledge of the therapist is of this second kind. It is during these moments of disarticulation of conscious attention, or during the moments of silence, that the therapist opens himself or herself to the patient's "entering." I readily acknowledge that the eloquence of silence—or the value of "not paying attention"—might be disputed by many writers, particularly those who place great emphasis on the importance of the verbal exchange, taken at its face value and responded to at that level. However, there is a growing interest in the metaphorical significance of patients' words that is, in turn, echoing Freud's discovery of symbol formation, condensation of themes, and similar features of free association. But the fact remains that some patients and therapists do not permit anything but a very small interval of silence to develop during the hour. In certain cases, talking itself becomes one of the more serious diversions from deeper therapeutic matters that never emerge in the verbal exchange.

Let me return to my main theme, the "incidental" thinking of the therapist, either while the patient speaks or during silences. This thinking appears to me, distinct and "beyond" countertransference, to be a greatly underrated vehicle for therapeutic understanding. Given this conviction, I have come to try to disarticulate my own thinking from any direct connection with the content of the patient's speech. This strategy came about as a result of a similar process involved in the treatment of young children in expressive play therapy.

Children, particularly below the ages of 6 or 7, express themselves almost entirely in symbols, metaphors, or fantasies. These are couched as stories, play scenes, dream material, and other forms of "pretend." To the child, and to some degree to the child therapist treating a child, pretense and reality are not always clearly distinguished one from another. Words do not have a consensually agreed-on meaning. The child and the therapist wander together in the mysterious third area of the mind.

Adults are much more verbally inclined and better served by secondary mechanisms (reasoning, logic, intellect); they are "better defended." These same secondary mechanisms are used to retain a precarious grasp of "reality" even in the therapeutic hour when the patient has the opportunity to examine his or her "unrealities," distortions of reality, or fantasies.

I alluded earlier to the example of the thought occurring to me during therapy that I am dying for a cup of tea. Or I may find my mind returning to a scene from childhood—a birthday party, for example—or I may wonder, somewhat more prosaically, what I will eat for dinner, or find myself thinking about a vacation. Is this unconscionable self-indulgence on my part or is there a place for this almost-daydreaming state in the treatment of patients? I would like to advance a dual hypothesis: that (a) these thoughts are beyond the usual concept of countertransference but are nevertheless a vital aspect of the therapist-patient interaction; and that (b) these thoughts represent my own mind's excursions into what Balint called the "third area"—excursions that are necessary for my bringing back into the direct exchange with the patient creative and helpful interpretation.

Paradoxically, it seems that when my mind is in this "peripheral" mode of thinking, I allow the patient the most direct access to private areas of my mind.

I have used this technique in clinical supervisions for some years, and it is from this arena that I derive the strongest evidence for its value. For example, when I would find, during the supervision of a close friend and colleague, that I persistently imagined myself lying on a beach snoozing, I discovered that she herself was hardly able to stay awake during the therapy hour with this particular child. I did not appear affected by the same imaginary scenes when she would present other children to me, and she would feel sleepy only with this particular child. She had dismissed the phenomenon as due to after-lunch sleepiness, although it occurred only on the day this child was seen. Our examination of our sleepiness unveiled previously unsuspected elements of this child's experience: that he had had certain terrifying (real) experiences which only sleep could anesthetize him against.

This example is quite simplistic compared with the types of understanding with which one can return from these journeys into the hinterlands of one's own associations. Although the third type of activity in the therapist's mind seems solipsistic and to consist of autochthonous ideas separate from the patient's associations, it may in fact contain the way around certain types of countertransference block. There is a reverie during which much valuable therapeutic work between the patient and the therapist occurs.

It is in the therapist's ability to descend and ascend between these levels of conscious and preconscious association that the therapeutic hour is made to assume its deeper integrative function. It might be more accurate to say that by retaining one foot in the world of reality and the other foot in the world of fantasy, the therapist allows the patient the possibility of crossing safely between the two worlds using the therapist as a bridge.

11

The Therapist's Contribution in the Reparative Process

In this chapter I am principally concerned with the therapist's direct influence on the child and of the child on the therapist during the play therapy hours. As a prelude, however, I will mention some contextual aspects of the play therapy situation that constitute highly formative indirect influences of the therapist on the child's situation.

INDIRECT THERAPEUTIC INFLUENCES

First, the therapist influences the community through his or her role as the representative of a body of specialized knowledge. Parents often think and worry for quite some time (a year or two is not uncommon) about the decision to seek help for their child before actually taking the step of making the telephone call for a consultation. During that "gestation" period, they build a relationship with the therapist through his or her reputation. In this sense the knowledge and reputation of the therapist in the community is the first step in the treatment of the child. The effectiveness of the therapy is, in part, predicated on the healthy gestation and nurturance of the parents' quest for help for their child. The care with which the suggestion for professional help is made is an important direction-setting part of the whole process of child therapy.

There is a particular emotional tone, an interpersonal stance, which some people are able to take, that both appreciates the parents' suffering in the presence of their child's difficulties and also questions the necessity of its continuing indefinitely. The person who recommends the consultation is saying that from his or her own knowledge "help is available somewhere" and also perhaps that vicissitudes of the child's character development can render the most concerned parenting ineffective. The referral process is not one that I understand well, except that I have become impressed by the importance (in the success of the therapy) of the tone that is set before I actually see the parent or the child.

Second, the therapist has an important indirect influence on the child through the restoration of the parents' hope and normal self-esteem. Parents who are dominated by their own and their child's combined bad objects tend to feel beleaguered, guilty, self-reproachful, angry, and sad. They are also assailed by induced feelings of helplessness, inadequacy, and sometimes futility, which will be discussed more fully later in my consideration of counter-transference effects in play therapy and play therapy supervision. I will only mention here the great store that I have come to set on making it possible for parents to be seen as "good enough" (Winnicott 1971b) by their children through restoring their ordinary sense of their own competence and sufficiency.

Third, the therapist can have an impact on the way the child is understood by and treated by the schoolteacher, who may have many observations but who probably does not have the luxury of either a comprehensive developmental history or a number of hours spent alone with the child, both of which are critical in understanding the child's special needs. Teachers play a large part in offering the child ego-oriented, development-promoting experiences in the classroom. However, difficult children, or children who are not overtly difficult to manage but are nevertheless in some hidden distress (e.g., the quiet, withdrawn child), may require special attention, which exceeds what can reasonably be expected of a classroom teacher.

The distraction of inner preoccupations, or of a rampant and vivid fantasy life, can turn the child's attention inward to the point that very little external reality actually enters the child's domain of consciousness. In these cases, no matter how much extra effort is made by a teacher, the child's window on the world is open only a fraction of what is necessary for effective learning in the classroom. Cameron (1972) has pointed out that there is an intimate association between learning difficulties and more general ego-constriction, fearfulness, lack of healthy narcissism, and poorly invested sublimation mechanisms.

Consequently, the therapist's consultations with the child's current and former teachers offer a two-way clinical advantage. First, these consultations permit a more comprehensive diagnostic formulation by the therapist, using the added information provided by the teachers. Second, they allow the therapist to communicate appropriately discreet knowledge about the child's likely emotional reactions in the classroom; this helps the teacher to stimulate the child's thirst for knowledge in school.

MORE DIRECT INFLUENCES

Nonverbal Influences

It will be seen from the protocols presented and from the earlier discussion that the therapist's influence during the treatment hours is largely, although not entirely, nonverbal. The therapist, in providing the place and the implicit opportunity for the child to communicate through play, fosters a profound style of partly regressive self-expression by the child. Several preliminary examples will dramatize this phenomenon.

Example 1. A child with no previous experience of play therapy entered the consulting room for the first time, constructed a complex World, and told a story about it to the therapist, who made no verbal contribution at all.

Example 2. A beginning child therapist requested a direct consultation on a "resistant" child who had "refused" to take any part in expressive play for some long period of time (months). The child came into the playroom where the therapist and consultant were present, immediately went to the sand tray, and made an elaborate World on which he worked for half an hour. Not a word was said to the child before he had completed most of the World.

Winnicott (1958, 1971a) demonstrates this process with many

of his clinical illustrations. It is as if a child reads the therapist's mind vis-à-vis "knowing what to do" in expressing himself or herself. One aspect of the therapist's direct influence on the child, then, is *allowing oneself to be read by the child.*

Influence of the Play Environment

This "reading" naturally includes not only the therapist personally but also the environment of the waiting room as well as the playroom, its equipment, and its availability to the child. Many playrooms in public and private clinics are extremely poorly equipped. The miniatures in one playroom I examined were at a height of 6 feet 6 inches over the sand tray, so the children could barely see them and had to ask the therapist to hand them down. Another contained a sand tray and fewer than a dozen miniatures in all. A third had a heap of toys thrown onto shelves as if on their way to the garbage. Often these playrooms were shared by several therapists, no one of whom felt responsible to correct the sad state of the rooms. Since the playroom is part of what is internalized by the child, its organization and contents must be carefully designed and maintained.

Influence of the Therapist's Mind

To return to the influence of the therapist per se, it should be noted that the child's ability to begin the therapeutic work is facilitated by the therapist's reticence and/or silence; what is helpful to the child is the lack of any direct mandate from the therapist about the nature of the play. Balint (1968) refers to a "third area" of the mind, in which creative forces are at work; he states explicitly that in his view it is in silence that the patient communicates with this part of his or her mind. He also points out that at the level of the "basic fault" (Balint's phrase for the part of the mind occupied by the patient's core conflicts), adult language is often useless because words do not always have an agreed upon meaning.

Guntrip (cited in Mackie 1969) has noted that the traditional psychoanalytic techniques of passivity and silence can be used by the analyst to project schizoid unrelatedness. Here we may usefully discriminate between a receptive and a rejecting silence. These gradually learned therapeutic techniques contribute to the establishment of the "facilitating environment" (Winnicott 1965).

The techniques are only partly extrapsychic. Bergson (1912) pointed out two different ways of knowing: we move around an object or we enter into it. The child's understanding of the therapist and of the therapeutic process (through the therapist) is of the second kind.

The "facilitating environment" is a safe place in the therapist's mind that the child can psychologically occupy. Winnicott (1965) uses this concept to denote an aspect of the parent-infant relationship that includes not only the actual holding of the infant but also the total environmental provision prior to the concept of *living with*. The play therapist, by allowing anamnestic regression, permits access to any historical period in the child's past.

Khan (1969) reiterates that the analyst's contribution to the establishment of the therapeutic rapport lies in the absence of interpretation. Khan also alludes to two vital aspects of recovery:

1. The patient's ability to allow an elaboration in fantasy promotes the patient's emotional development and recovery.
2. The patient depends on the therapist to recognize the patient's need to be in the suffering state—without needing overt help or intervention.

I will return momentarily to consider these points in turn. First, however, it is necessary to consider another piece of evidence of the therapeutic effect. In both the cases presented in this study, and in the majority of others not included in this work, rapid relief in the parent-child dimensions of the conflict occurred. Symptomatic relief in real life occurs long before the emergence of the reparative motif. How can so rapid an effect be explained?

Dolto (1947) observed the reactions of a child (Jean) soon after the birth of a sibling. Dolto observed the child's confusion, expressed by bed-wetting, soiling, and stammering. The symptoms stopped on the twenty-first day after the birth, when Jean put a celluloid doll, whom he named Guicha (his new brother's name), in the maid's bed and "killed" it in his mother's presence. Then he immediately began to act in gentle and solicitous ways toward both the doll and the baby. His stammering, soiling, and wetting ceased. Dolto points out the crucial distinction here between the murderous intention and the murderous fantasy, the latter actually being a manifestation of love.

Wax (1973) also shows the important difference between pretending and intention; he goes so far as to suggest that the ability to pretend (or in its natural absence, being taught how to pretend) can mean the difference between psychosis and health. Wax made these observations while studying the recovery of a child he was treating at the Reiss-Davis Child Study Center in Los Angeles. The child, 6 years old and thought to have borderline personality organization, played out themes that in their repetition, "bore an uncanny resemblance to the ancient myth of Daedalus and Icarus" (p. 301). The child was terrified by his mental images of giant monsters and the idea of being carried aloft by a giant kite (evidently allowing him a sense of escape). He also "cooked himself in a pretend oven," saying to Dr. Wax, "You are going to eat me up," and adding after a pause, "Just pretend!" (p. 301). Wax's participation in this imaginary feast allowed the child to include his own worst fear into a "pretend" situation.

We see then that play, as these authors and I have reported it, takes the place of a dreaded reality. The child, in the absence of the play therapy situation, manipulates the parents unconsciously to adopt roles in a psychodrama in which the child's worst fantasies are recapitulated. Mackie (1969) has alluded to the almost delusional "reality" the recipient of a projective identification feels. This situation (namely, that of the child vis-à-vis the parents) prolongs the child's fantastic dilemma.

The early play therapy sessions act in concert with the child's fantasy productions to trap and express, to and *through* the therapist, the fearsome or problematic foci the child is attempting to master.

THE REVIVAL AND SHARING OF
PRIMITIVE FANTASIES

The creation of a play scene by the child in play therapy initiates two processes of unconscious fantasy: one in the child and one in the therapist. The process in the child will often be reported (by the child or the parents) to have continued in the child's dreams during the nights between the play sessions. The process in the therapist can be observed in the therapist's dreams, in "idle" daytime thoughts, and, of course, in daydreams. The child's world can come to life and be animated in the child's and in the therapist's dreams. One mother, who attended a lecture I once gave on play therapy, decided to try a play technique I had discussed on her child, who was having nightmares. The very night following the day she tried the Squiggle Game she herself began to have nightmares that would not "leave her alone" in the daytime. Only after therapeutic intervention were both she and the child able to release their nightmare-creating fantasies.

THERAPEUTIC INTIMACY AND DISTANCE

I will now add to Khan's suggestions. The child's and the parents' inability to allow the terrifying elaboration in fantasy of already too terrifying object conflicts creates a fixation in the child, which in turn causes family processes to degenerate further. The therapist's intervention consists of allowing a "playground" in which this elaboration can occur. This process is enhanced by the therapist's ability to offer a certain kind of "middle distance" relationship, which allows the child to enter these dark regions and to lead the therapist there. In the early hours of play therapy the slightest physical absence of the therapist is a staggering blow to the child. When I once stepped momentarily outside my playroom, the play was immediately put away, and I knew from the child's reactions that this had been a terrible shock.

On the other hand, too intrusive or involved a presence also seems to impair the delicate unfolding process that the child brings to the therapy. In the first minutes of seeing a child I try to divine what emotional and physical distance seems right for the child in question. Some children want and need me to be inches away from them, whereas others are better served if I am across the room, engrossed in my own thoughts.

Mackie (1969) also described the necessity to serve patients according to their emotional needs for intimacy or distance. Khan (1969) gives several examples of the patient's *use* of the analyst in the clinical situation. He also emphasizes the importance of allowing this "using" to occur.

The child's use of the therapist is regressively amplified in the transference to a task of life-saving importance.

A CONTRASTING TECHNIQUE

I have underlined the nondiscursive elements that determine the therapist's involvement with the child. This approach should be contrasted with that of Gardner (1971), who, after the child makes up a story in which there are traumatic themes, invents a similar story with somewhat more positive themes. In a sense he offers the child an alternative solution to the problems that the story poses. In my view, Gardner offers alternate defensive formulations to the child, but I am not convinced that this intervention actually addresses the child's central problems.

Although Gardner tends not to report the nondiscursive elements of his treatment of children concurrently with his overt techniques, Gardner offers the child an opportunity to develop his or her own reparative formulations through the unconscious borrowing of Gardner's resources. My own explorations into formulating reparative solutions for children have had different results from Gardner's. The following example will illustrate this difference.

A child whom I saw had had a very disturbed infancy; he was described by several observers outside the family as "the most difficult baby" they had seen. In her adolescence, his mother had

had suicidal depressions. This child was making a World. His World showed a scene in which it was very nearly the end of the world. Even Superman was dying. "If Superman does not move in one minute," the child said, "it will be too late. He will be dead and the world will come to an end. . . . Sixty. Fifty-nine. Fifty-eight. . . . Ten. Nine. Eight. . . ."

When the count reached three, I could stand it no longer. Something bordering on panic overcame me, and I picked up a tiny fluffy bird. "Superbirdie is here," I said, and Superbirdie gave Superman a life-saving injection in the arm. With noticeably diminished enthusiasm, the child had Superman save the earth. Then he said, "Now the world is coming to an end. Superman is dying and, this time *Superbirdie is out of town!*" (the child's emphasis).

This time I understood that in rescuing the child from his pretend disaster I had probably stood in the way of his therapy at that moment. In the repetition the child devised his own solution. The count stopped at one and, many seconds later, Superman got up and saved the world. He had generated the reparative motif he wanted. I had forgotten one of my own sayings to children, "In make-believe anything can happen." In this child's make-believe world, the doomsday clock became stuck at one second, allowing Superman any amount of time to save the world.

To return briefly to Gardner's technique, it may be that he is more able than I to sense what play themes the child can accept in gradually approaching the reparative moment. Or it may be that Gardner-and-the-child become the psychological entity who, as a union, generate their reparative motif. As is evident from the protocols, I incline more toward Laing's view of the therapist's function. Laing (1961) insists that the basic function of the therapy is to provide a setting in which as little as possible impedes the patient's capacity to discover his or her own self. He emphasizes that the therapist must not only be adaptable but must also be scrupulously honest in intention—by remaining free from any sort of impingement or prejudicing of the patient in favor of the therapist's solution to the patient's difficulty.

THE TRUE AND THE FALSE SELF

The reasons for this approach come in part from a wish to avoid contributing to the development or entrenchment of a "false self" behind which compliant facade the individual hides. Guntrip (1968) described the two sides of the personality of disturbed individuals: the *visible* side—that is, the devitalized conscious self tending toward depersonalization; and the *invisible* side—that is, a "retreat of the vital heart of the psyche to a secret 'safe inside' position" (p. 42). This retreat is graphically shown in Christine's painting, "My hearts" (see Fig. 8, Chapter 7). These ideas of Guntrip's are an extension of Fairbairn's (1952) approach to endopsychic structure in object relations terms. Guntrip adumbrates a splitting process that occurs in the self, so that there is (a) a regressed libidinal ego that retires to the innermost depths of the psyche and can remain out of reach for a lifetime; and (b) an oral, sadomasochistic libidinal ego that remains tied to and active in the bad object domain of the internal world. This formulation is clearly shown in the dualistic themes of Jennifer's stories, the oral sadomasochistic themes being especially clear.

These manifestations and their resolution in play therapy will be considered theoretically in the next chapter, with special reference to the role of the play and of the play therapist as transitional objects.

THE PARALLEL WITH
SOMATIC IMMUNE MECHANISMS

These theoretical formulations now permit a fuller delineation of the parallel between the somatic processes of pathogenesis (and its associated immune response) and the corresponding psychological process. (These ideas were introduced at the end of Chapter 8.) Babies at birth are already equipped with some degree of immune response, although individual differences do occur. These differences range from an effective immune system to immune deficiency disease, which requires that the child be encapsulated in a protective shield until the immune system develops. In the body's immune response the possibly dangerous, invading organisms (antigens) are recognized by the body as alien (requiring a capacity for self/not-self discrimination) and are neutralized by the creation of complementary, opposite molecules (see Figure 26).

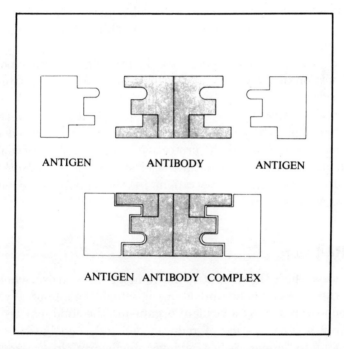

Figure 26. Antigens and the creation of complementary, opposite molecules. *Top:* The evidence indicates that an antibody molecule has two identical halves, each composed of one large component and one small component. *Bottom:* The two active surfaces of the antibody molecule probably fit against the active surfaces of two antigen molecules, thus masking and inactivating them. (Copyright © Norton. Reprinted by permission.)

Antibody Creation

It is the nature of the antigen itself that determines the antibody created and also the antigen-specificity of each antibody. However, when the immune system has once recognized an invader and created the neutralizing antibody, it readily responds to future attacks by the same organism, so that many childhood diseases are "caught" only once. The progressive stimulation of the immune system actually increases its repertoire of antibody response, reducing the likelihood of *any* infection. This phenomenon is used prophylactically by vaccination, in which a mild version of a pathogen (e.g., heat-killed bacterial strains) is deliberately introduced to stimulate the immune response.

There is a clear analogy here with the role of graduated exposure to frustration in the young infant; this stimulates the development of frustration-tolerating (and I would now add *reparative*) mechanisms. Excessively protected infants do indeed show severe adverse reactions when in later life they suddenly are faced with problems away from their protective sphere—the first day of school, for example. The natural vicissitudes of an infant's life generally provide ample frustrations for the satisfactory development of some reparative mechanisms.

The Rest Cure

In cases where the reparative mechanism has been overwhelmed (as in the case of somatic infections in which the immune system has been overcome by a virulent organism), the child may recover if simply given a period of reduced demands and burdens (the equivalent to "going to bed and keeping warm" in the somatic case). The psychological trauma, however, may remain as a latent weakness, walled off by structuring elements of the personality. Occasionally, pockets of physical infection may remain in the body only to burgeon at another time of physical (*or emotional*) stress. These regressive solutions (being taken care of, going to bed) do sometimes work comprehensively.

The play therapy relationship has many elements of sufficiently reducing the stress on the child to allow the formulation of neutralizing antibody or reparative responses. As in the physical case, however, some more dramatic intervention is sometimes necessary.

Transfer Factor

One of the newer treatment techniques for certain persistent failures of the immune response is the use of transfer factor, in which a substance (or factor) that creates immunity in a healthy individual is extracted from that individual and injected into a sick individual. The psychological parallel is here a little closer to a metaphor. The use of transfer factor requires the donation of some of the restitutive strengths of a healthy individual in the service of fighting the illness of the suffering individual.

In the course of play therapy the phenomenon of the assimilation and modification of aspects of the child's traumatic fantasies by the therapist's unconscious reparative processes may be seen in the therapist's dreams and fantasy life. This parallel also is seen in Gardner's technique. Whether consciously planned or unconsciously occurring, it seems legitimate to postulate the *borrowing* of the therapist's libidinal and reparative resources in the course of the child's recovery.

Antibiotic Administration

The last parallel that will be drawn between the somatic and the psychological recovery processes is in the use of antibiotics, which only inactivate certain bacterial infections. This parallel is perhaps the weakest of all but nonetheless worth considering. We need to think of the ways in which certain psychological traumas may be readily "removed" by the administration of a "broad-spectrum" therapeutic agent. We might think in this instance of the traumatic neuroses of childhood which, as severe as the precipitating trauma might be, respond favorably to cathartic play or even to educational efforts. The disadvantage of these approaches lies in

their failure to advance the sophistication of the reparative mechanisms, possibly leaving the child more vulnerable to subsequent
traumatization. The physical analog, physical habituation, tends not
to occur in individuals exposed to repeated administration of antibiotics, but the bacterial pool does develop resistant, and therefore
more dangerous, strains.

Further theoretical consideration of the internal psychological
processes of reparation will now be undertaken.

12
Reparation in the Family Constellation

When I present my work to professional meetings in California, where the influence of the "Family Therapy" treatment paradigm is widespread, I have come to anticipate the reaction bordering on incredulity to the fact that I successfully treat children to the satisfaction of their parents, teachers, and other observers without ever treating the parents in their own right. Many analytic colleagues view young children as best treated by seeing the parents or the mother. I use a treatment model that regards having a child as perhaps the definitive event in family functioning. Events may supervene that disarticulate the healthy family development, and these events can be extrinsic to the family or internal as a prenatal event affecting the baby in utero. I have come to have greater and greater respect for the impact of prenatal medical interventions, from the way pregnancy is discovered and announced to the parents, to the attitude of the obstetric/gynecological staff and the procedures and ambience of delivery itself. M. P. M. Richards (1979) and Michel Odent (1976), although somewhat different in their views, have contributed to our knowledge about this early critical period of psychological development of the family.

My premise is that from the moment the child is conceived, the different members of a family "lead one life" psychologically. However good or bad conscious communication between the family members is, they share an emotional existence: they coexist psychologically.

I will add parenthetically that these family members (those of the family of procreation) coexist psychologically with their families of origin, including living and dead members. The antecedence of psychological determination is thus lost in the mists of time.

In regard to this coexistence, it can be said that the family as a

183

whole becomes dominated by bad objects and that the child, the most vulnerable and "exposed" member, most clearly expresses this domination. I would like to go further to say I believe that the families of babies and young children become dominated by the baby's or child's bad objects—that is, they are unable to contain the bad objects in the baby's mind within the matrix of the family's good object system. The family's love is overwhelmed by the child's primitive hate, so the whole family becomes "ill."

By restoring the child's developmental course to more moderate limits, acting myself as a container transitionally, I give the parents a chance to recover their own mature functioning.

I will elaborate this model and return to the question of how parents' own psychological needs are brought into the child treatment situation.

The Case of the Disappearing Kangaroo, by Sherlock Bones

One day, in the depths of the forest, three kangaroos were hopping along. One of the kangaroos said: "Let's go down to the waterbank." The others agreed. There were two grown-up kangaroos and one younger kangaroo. After they had gotten to the waterbank, the father came to them and said: "Now let's all jump in." "But it's too cold" said the mother and the child. As they walked away, father grumbled to himself: "**##***$$$$%%%%." The others hopped and skipped to where they had a picnic waiting for them. So they skipped along as if they had no worry in the world. But the sky grew darker and it looked like rain. Father still wanted to swim. Mother Kangaroo said, "Come on, we must go home. It is about to rain. You can go swimming tomorrow." So they quickly packed up their food and put up their umbrellas. Getting wet as they walked home, Baby Kangaroo said, "I wish this rain would stop." Just then Daddy Kangaroo was hit by lightning and vanished into thin air.

The child who told this story, now a 12-year-old girl, had experienced a period of paternal absence when she was a baby. When the father (who had been serving abroad in the armed forces) returned, she was unable to reconnect to him. She began to lie (or at any rate confabulate) and for many years had little to do with him in spite of his receptivity and overtures to her. She had become involved in petty delinquency, shoplifting, and so on. The family was functioning, but a part of its emotional life had been blocked. The child's fixation distorted the ordinary flow of emotions between the family members. The child continued the story in a way that indicates dissolution of this fixation, as will be seen at the end of this chapter.

The rectification in the child's mind of the fixated "disappeared daddy" idea, the reparative motif that he was only gone for a while (it just seemed like forever), allowed a restoration of complete and balanced family functioning. Delinquent manifestations ceased.

I will first address the complex question of how family constellations affect (and are affected by) children, particularly the unusually sensitive or vulnerable children we see in play therapy.

The family of every child in play therapy undergoes a change in the family constellation to meet the new dynamic situation that therapy occasions. The emotional state of families seeking play therapy for a child is frequently at or close to the breaking point. The disturbance induced in such a metastable family system by the powerful medicine of play therapy for a child is more than enough to "make or break" the stability of the family constellation.

It is therefore a common aspect of a child therapist's work to struggle to examine and understand the effects of the changing family constellation on the child, and the effects "having this child" has had on the couple.

Children, even as babies, exert powerful, usually unconscious and unacknowledged influences on their parents' emotional life. I propose therefore to devote some effort to addressing the role of the child's instinctual development on the mental stability and the emotional lives of her or his parents or stepparents.

My direction, which places great weight on object relations theory, takes me inside the child's mind rather than focusing on overt aspects of family relations. My treatment model takes advantage of this theory by attempting to work at the deepest, most primitive levels of human emotions in the child. I do not leave it to nature to effect contingent change in the parents. By working at the level of unconscious fantasy in the child, I also produce significant change in the family arrangements at this level of unconscious fantasy.

In these days of weakened social repression mechanisms, instinctual processes, subtle as they can sometimes be, exert a more dramatic influence than when the social order was more rigid. For example, oedipal pressures from a child toward a parent more readily lead to the expression with an outside partner of the forbidden incestuous drives felt toward the child. The outside relationship is then rationalized, and may indeed be "needed." An extramarital affair is surely preferable to incest. I am speaking now, of course, in the simplistic and overdetermined logic of the unconscious.

My sense is that there is currently an inadequate recognition or understanding of the instinctual pressures between child and parent that lead to marital discord or psychological dysfunction in one or the other parent.

Recent research has shown that the emotional circumstances of conception and early pregnancy become a template for subsequent family functioning. The response of the couple to the presence of a "third party" or third member in the family predicts, or even predestines, the development of the family for years to come. At the moment of conception, even as an "idea," the child determines many aspects of subsequent family functioning. Interviews of newly pregnant primiparous couples (Stauthamer 1982) have shown how powerful an influence this tiny being becomes as soon as her or his existence is detected.

If we are to be consistent, we need to view the child's "family" as including all the emotionally important people, all the "relatives," current, former, and future, with which each parent is, has been, or will be involved. Through the parents, these all become significant "objects" in the child's object world.

The theory of object relations allows us to explain and predict the impact between children and the family constellation. Let me digress for a moment from my description of object relations theory. The problem we are examining from the child's point of view is similar to that of studying a meeting between two persons from different lands who have different traditions and languages.

My analogy is closest for those children who, growing up in one family, have to adapt to a new family after a divorce, but it applies equally to the child who is born into a family with a history of earlier marriage in either or both members of the couple. Those who have traveled in countries where they did not know the language will know at firsthand the experience to which I am alluding.

Let me describe a small personal vignette that forcefully brought the point home to me. One summer I stayed in Basel, visiting friends in Switzerland. Basel is in German-speaking Switzerland but is less than 15 minutes from Mulhouse, a small town in northeastern France between Burgundy and Alsace. Although everyone in Basel speaks English, my inability to speak German led me to feel stupid, inarticulate, angry, depressed, and impatient except when I was with my friends. However, I could walk into France and find myself readily able to communicate sensitively and effectively with almost anyone. I was restored to my own sense of personal identity. One of my presuppositions, therefore, is that for children to feel themselves, they must be able to make themselves *understandable* to the family culture. I am referring now not only to the spoken language but to gesture, belief system, values, and all the other means by which we represent our humanity to one another.

Let me now return to the theoretical part. In order to examine the influence of diverse family constellations on a child, we need to agree on a model, a paradigm, for the influence of the outside world on the child. That is to say, we need a model of *internalization*. To what processes do we attribute the determination of a child's personality? A simple representation of the factors is shown in Figure 27. Various elements—endopsychic, biological, societal

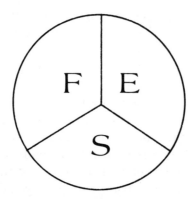

Figure 27. The influences on a child. *F*, familial factors; *S*, social factors; *E*, endopsychic factors.

(social relations, economic factors, the national "mood," parental factors)—interact to contribute to the personality influences on the child. The proportion of each may vary widely.

In Europe there tends to be more emphasis on the child's individuality exerting itself, whereas in the United States more emphasis is given to the effect of the parent's relationship style on the child's difficulties. However, even in the United States there is wide variation in the sense of responsibility that parents have for their child's development. I have sensed that a phenomenon occurs in the parents of nervous or difficult children who are presented for treatment: Parents who worry at all about their influence on a particular child tend to exaggerate their responsibility and perhaps even become too paralyzed to exert any influence at all. On the other hand, parents who tend to be less concerned about their influence on their child or children go to an extreme in that direction, abandoning any attempt to modulate their involvement with the child. In effect both of these tendencies produce the same result: an absence of balanced parent–child interaction.

By exaggerating the possiblities inherent in their role as parents, many parents underestimate the power of processes out of their control (their own unconscious, biology, society) and thus tend to feel guilty over processes not in fact subject to their influence. Their omnipotent ideas of parenthood are challenged, and they lapse into helplessness.

How are the social and parental factors taken in by the child?

Let me briefly recapitulate the theory of internalization of "objects," mental representations of the real world as it is perceived and distorted by the child. Klein tried to describe how babies perceive the world and record its influence in their character. The breast, we could probably agree, is a vital, warm, nourishing, and comforting object that gives pleasures and satisfaction to the child: a "good object" in its internalization.

Colicky pain, or fright, or a period of maternal absence, are all examples of experiences that would be taken in as "bad objects." There are also objects with varying degrees of goodness or badness that have varied emotional connotations.

Transference is the introduction of aspects of the early relationships (between, for example, the baby and the breast) as distortions into later relationships, including the relationship with the mother herself. For example, a baby with feeding difficulties in the first month of life subsequently may project a "depriving breast" onto the mother. Thereafter the baby fails to respond to her then "adequate mothering," seeing her instead as a highly ambivalent or even depriving object. This primitive aspect of the earliest relationship will enter all other relationships, including the relationship to the whole outside world.

There is a very complex arrangement of objects with good, bad, and intermediate objects in a structure theorists call the ego structure. The personality extends indefinitely in all directions. The relationship of these internal objects to the ego structure is comparable to the relationship of a person to external reality. The ego structure can be fluid or even disorganized, or it can be rigid and very organized.

In considering the child's personality we need to know, most simply, the content of the internal objects (threatening, nurturing, angry, greedy, and so on) and how they are organized.

Where do internal objects come from and what are they? The ultimate origin of internal objects is through introjection, and they consist of internal mental structures that *represent* (re-present) emotionally significant aspects of persons on whom the child depends early in life. These internal representatives undergo considerable, even *great* elaboration and distortion at the instance of the individual's own needs and emotions. Thus, internal objects are far from being mere images or reflections of the outside world. For example, a breast that might be, in all real senses, adequately nurturing may be taken in as a bad, depriving object by a child who is in a mood of frightening, insatiably voracious hunger.

I have so far described "the child" as if we know where the child begins and the mother ends. This is problematic during pregnancy, when there is a continuous physical entity—mother-and-child—and after birth when there is a continuous psychological entity—child-and-the-rest-of-the-world. I have already alluded in Chapter 2 to the idea (put forward by Margaret Mahler and others) of the child's gradual individuation, as a personality boundary forms between self and others.

However, in my view this boundary is never clearly defined; adults no more than children possess firm boundaries. This idea comes from the studies on group dynamics by Bion (1970), Ezriel (1950), Foulkes (1957), and others. Perhaps, more accurately, it is not that there are *no* boundaries but that boundaries are changeable, dynamic, and fluid; and emotions or emotional states can cross the boundaries quite readily. The clearest example of this is seen in couples or people in love, in whom it is hard to say which affects belong to which person. There is a substantial degree of fusion or dissolution of personal boundaries in these instances and also in many of the ordinary transactions of everyday life.

I can illustrate the importance of this phenomenon in considering the child's internalization of the breast. The child's experience at the breast depends in part on the mother's experience of the child at the breast, and simultaneously of aspects of herself in the outside world. The mother acts as the bearer to the child of emotional news from the outside world. If she is secure, content, well loved, if she has the lineaments of gratified desire, she will offer the child a different experience than if she is angry, depressed, or feeling unsupported.

The "mother" is herself a complex object system, with a mosaic of more and less organized parts, and more and less loving parts. So is the father, the grandparents, or any other individuals in the child's experience. From birth the child is exposed to a complex, continuous object field that is diverse both historically and in contemporary social influences. We each have daily experiences of temporary introjection and of identifications that affect our moods and have an influence on who we are for a little while. An argument with the boss leaves us a different person than does a visit to the theater.

The child's experience of the people he or she internalizes is thus heterogeneous. It is not strictly people who are internalized but relationships, people viewed through the distorting lens of the child's relationship with them.

The family is a chimera, an organism formed by genetically mixing two individuals in a couple that includes but goes beyond their individual personalities. A chimera includes the genetic characteristics of each contributing species in some more or less compatible combination. Let me reflect for a moment on this idea of "compatibility." As I mentioned earlier, each individual is a mosaic of more or less compatible parts. Some individuals are, of course, full of internal conflict, at odds with themselves.

The child's relationship with the "couple" who are his or her original parents depends on the degree to which the family members operate together (*cooperate*) or to the degree to which they function dissonantly, at odds with one another. To use my analogy of my experience in Basel: Are both parents speaking a shared language or is the child required to switch between languages to communicate with each parent? Are the internalized parents at odds with one another? In the case of multiple family constellations, how well do all the members of the constellation operate together?

In the case of an unstable couple, clearly disharmonious or disconnected independent functioning is present, and it will be a challenge to the child's versatility to organize a coherent system of personality.

We can predict that the children of divided families are, a priori, more likely to have experienced a problematic family constellation and more likely to have a balance weighed toward "bad objects" and to be less well organized internally.

The child's task is to synthesize the often contradictory aspects of the family members. Children in treatment present with an unbalanced object system—the matrix of love and hate within the child is "split," not in the sense of the split of schizophrenia, but in the sense of splitting as a polarization between love and hate, between one parent and the other, or between one part of the self and another. In extremis, the child may have retreated inside into a safe, secret inner corner while leaving a shallow, labile, and insubstantial outer "shell" self that relates to the real world. In the illustrations of Chapter 7 we see the emergence of the vital idea that objects can work together cooperatively to ward off predatory threat. Christine has been able to recruit from inside herself aspects from both parts of herself—the parts affiliated with each family—to redirect her aggression in an ego-syntonic direction; namely, to sustain her own life. This could occur only after she synthesized these opposed family structures in her mind.

This reparative theme is a general human preoccupation: in much art, literature, and music there is a descent to face fear followed by a triumphant revival of the spirit. This motif emerges in the same sequence in almost all of child and adult psychotherapy; it is perhaps the essence of the human struggle. The Martha Graham Dance Company has in its repertoire a piece entitled "Errand into the Maze." The theme of this piece epitomizes the nature of the struggle for personal integration: "There is an errand into the maze of the heart's darkness to do battle with the Creature of Fear. There is the accomplishment of the errand, the instant of triumph, and the emergence from the dark." You will see this motif echoed in my other examples as well as in memories that come to mind of your own work. What we seek in family restructuring, of course, is the emergence of this theme: the battle with and triumphant victory over the Creature of Fear.

Here are some brief vignettes that illustrate the nature of the Creature of Fear, its impact on the child and family, and the emergence of the family from fear when the trauma was released through play therapy with the child. The first illustration shows how the child's treatment neutralized a terrifying family specter concerning the destructive nature of sexual love.

When Luke was 7 months old, his mother had a lover whom she had met on a brief trip. This relationship, passionate enough, was destined to be short-lived. When Luke was 9 months old, some eight weeks into the affair, Luke's father went out of town for a few days. During these few days Luke's mother's lover shot himself in the head and killed himself. Luke's father was apprised of the situation when he returned.

An association in fantasy between passionate sexual love and death was established. When Luke was brought for treatment some three years later, the presenting complaint was "He is missing a way of relating to people that is intimate" and "He has no sympathy for other people's feelings and problems." The parents had separated by then and were living in rancorous estrangement.

In Handel's *Giulio Cesare*, Cleopatra, fearing the death of her lover, Caesar, prays to the gods for mercy. She stands on Mount Parnassus, home of the gods, and sings

> If thou dost not feel mercy for me,
> just heaven, I will die.
> Give thou peace to my torment,
> or this soul will die.*

The whole family, Luke and his parents, had become terrified to love and terrified by love. They defensively sustained angry distance. Captured in the child's mind was the early scene, expressed in his first psychotherapy session thus: "The truck came through the tunnel. It smashed down the other truck and killed the monster" (cf. the "monster" theme in Chapter 7). He added, to complete the picture, "some people were out of town."

Through the vaginal tunnel of his mother two truck-penises had collided. The monster (sexual love between a man and a woman) was destroyed. "Some people" (the father himself) were out of town. But his image remained in the mother's, the child's, and the lover's minds.

---

*Copyright © 1967, RCA Records. Reproduced by permission.

The degree of tragedy crystallized in this family's group psyche produced a serious technical problem in retaining a balanced view during the treatment. It was at times difficult for me to retain my hopefulness. However, the child and the parents did recover after fairly protracted play therapy. The treatment of the child freed the parents from much of their own rage (some of which was directed toward me), and the mother later entered psychiatric treatment herself.

I want to be explicit in my conclusion here. The child's treatment in and of itself allowed both parents to recover a good part of their mental health. The resolution of the traumatic motif in the mind of the child restored hope to the family members and allowed the mother to seek her own treatment.

I will return to the allusion I made that the family rage became directed against me, for it introduced another important aspect of how parents use the child therapist for their own "treatment." Parents periodically discuss their child's reactions to my treatment, and any other concerns they have about that treatment. I am also rather strict about their coming on time to deliver and pick up the child from my office (which is in my home) and about regular payment of fees. These arrangements may not sound too demanding; however, they are the vehicle through which some parents express their difficulties to me. In Luke's case the mother's rage toward me was ostensibly because I did not take her side enough in the intense marital hostility and because she felt I was angry with her. The displacement of repressed feelings from her now long-dead lover is quite transparent.

In another case a very anxious parent managed to have an auto accident right outside my window. She had pulled out of her parking space just as another car was passing. A little later she called to ask what impact the chaotic life-style that she and her husband manifested was having on their 2½-year-old daughter, who was refusing to eat (and was in fact maintaining a weight at a dangerously low level). This family also had to be reminded about coming to collect their daughter on time and to pay my fees. So I was brought into the family chaos in many ways.

This phenomenon is most valuable in that it allows me to experience firsthand the "feel" of the family and my reactions to it. These management questions often have a great poignancy and present complex dilemmas for me. For example, one father brought his child at the beginning of the hour, having arranged for his now separated wife to pick up the child at the end of the session. I was incensed and amazed, about half an hour after the child had left, to find the father emerging from my bathroom saying that he hoped I did not mind his changing and shaving therein. My housekeeper later pointed out to me two empty beer bottles and an empty can of nuts in the bathroom wastebasket.

Here was a man who needed a home, or as he put it: "I need to change to go for an interview for a new apartment. I have to move."

These examples only touch on a very difficult area of child and adult interaction: the flow between regressive and progressive aspects of even the most mature self. This challenge offers itself broadly to the professional community of child therapists. A colleague in Berkeley, Dr. B., and I were consulted independently by the father and mother, respectively, of a severely disturbed and possibly psychotic child. The parents had been fighting since they met seven years earlier. They could cooperate on virtually nothing, and that is why they each sought a therapist for their child independently. Dr. B. and I thought we could synthesize our efforts to get both parents to trust one of us. Dr. B. wisely said she thought I should be the one. The outcome of the story is that I was still, after several weeks, trying to get the parents to agree on a time the child could come to see me. My latest information is that a judge has ordered the couple to "cooperate" with one another sufficiently to initiate the consultation with me.

I do not want to end on a note of such unfulfillment, and I must complete the story of the Disappearing Kangaroo and tell what happens to Cleopatra after her entreaty to the gods. In the last act of *Giulio Cesare*, with the tyrant Ptolemy vanquished and killed, Cleopatra's mood has changed: Caesar has come back and made her Queen of Egypt. She sings to him:

> When, broken by the storms,
> the ship comes safe to port,
> the sailor has no other desire.

> So the heart, torn with suffering and tears,
> when at last it is comforted,
> brings ecstasy anew to the soul.

Similarly, let me present the triumphant end of the story of the Disappearing Kangaroo, with which I began this chapter:

So they looked around for Daddy. They searched high and they searched low, but they could not find him. They were looking for half an hour, an hour, two hours. The rain was getting worse. Just as they had given up hope, Daddy popped down out of the tree where he had jumped, frightened by the lightning. "We thought you had disappeared," they all cried. "No," said the father, "I was just very scared so I jumped up in the tree. Now I'm back again." And they all went home and lived happily ever after.

13
Reparation through Transitional Processes

The work of play therapy has been described in this study as an unfolding by the child of a progressive message to the therapist, a message couched in the special language of play. The importance of the therapist's understanding of this language has not yet been considered. This understanding, and the child's ability to internalize one who has become a part of the child's play productions, is but one aspect of the therapist's role as a bridge for the child, standing between the child's split, conflicted parts. The therapist thus becomes a translating transitional object, speaking both the idiosyncratic language of the child's play and the language of the therapist's own developmental maturity.

In this chapter I will consider these functions in more detail, both as they are reflected in the play protocols and as they amplify our understanding of the features of reparation.

To recapitulate Klein's original idea of reparation, it is in the depressive phase, involving separation from the mother, that love is made angry. Children fear that the hate they feel will destroy the person they need for survival, and therefore they instinctively turn the hate inward against the self—as guilt and self-reproach.

Prior to the onset of the depressive position, in the so-called schizoid position (prior to the capacity for ambivalence), needy and frustrated love becomes so all-devouring that the fear is love, not hate, will consume and destroy the child's world. These themes are clearly evident in Jennifer's stories. The dilemma is more serious than in the depressive position. The child's increasing hunger for human contact as well as for food is felt to be so dangerous that he or she withdraws into indifference and futility (Barker and Schmidt 1971).

The successive stories in Jennifer's protocol illustrate the gradual emergence from this phase through the discovery (in play) of

199

imaginary resources to set against her imaginary hungry monsters. By contrast Christine hints at oral themes, but she more prominently reflects depressive anxiety and symptomatology. We can see the empty expanses in her first World (session 1); we sense simultaneously the attachment-separation conflicts in the two palm trees (scene 1) and in the saber-toothed tiger's quest to recover her lost cub (scene 3).

Mackie (1969) points out (in speaking of analytically oriented psychotherapy) that one of his patients regarded him initially more as a "home" than as a person. Somewhat later, she referred to him as "like a stake that a small tree is supported by" (p. 376). For a long period Mackie could not make out what he represented to her. "Eventually," Mackie reports, "it dawned on me that I was a transitional object. This was confirmed retrospectively much later when she acquired a teddy bear (never having had one in childhood) and said she realized that this was what I (or her idea of me) had been to her for a couple of years" (p. 376).

The formulation of the therapist as a transitional object can be widely interpreted in the play scenes illustrated in this study. The therapist represents both the cub-stealing but human cavemen *and* the wild but maternal, saber-toothed tiger in Jennifer's first session. In her story of Harry Hublick (who metamorphoses to Harolyn Hopeless) the therapist captures personifications both of hungry Harry and of satiated Scaley. In fact, the therapeutic relationship includes projective identifications of all the characters in the child's play. The therapist acts as a "container" for the child's objects as they are expressed through the play. Thus, therapists not only "enter" the child through their attempts to understand the play language, but they also allow the child to enter themselves. The therapist expropriates some of the child's conflicts, providing both subjective relief to the child and an improved opportunity for the recovery of the child's reparative mechanisms.

THE PROFESSIONAL ENVIRONMENT

Therapists take in the play themes (into memory and the clinical file) and unconsciously address these conflicted or desperate themes with their own personality mechanisms. The child and therapist might have alternating dreams that pick up and advance particular thematic lines in the play session. The effectiveness of therapists in this role depends on their own integrative strengths of personality and on their own professional stability, milieu, and supervision relationship—in other words, on the whole context of the therapeutic effort.

The clinical supervision of play therapists shows an overall structure, even to the progression through traumatic themes to a reparative motif. The supervision process mirrors that of the play therapist and child in their work together. The professional paradigm can be seen in terms of a libidinal transduction, beginning with the child's communication of distress to the therapist, continuing with the communication of the distress from the therapist to the clinical supervisor, and with some reparative processing at each step along the way. It is helpful to consider these processes from the heuristic viewpoint of the induced feelings in the play therapist faced with the child's many emotionally demanding projective identifications. (These observations come from my own experience with children and also from my discussions of child therapy cases as a consultant to some 12 less experienced play therapists in various professional disciplines.)

COUNTERTRANSFERENCE IN PLAY THERAPY AND IN PLAY THERAPY SUPERVISION

In the hours prior to the emergence of the reparative motif there is a stunning sense of discouragement, powerlessness, and inadequacy. These feelings not only affect the therapist but also presumably mirror something of what the child is feeling in the face of a system of persecutory or frightening fantasies. These may be the same kind of feelings that affect the child's parents, against which they have had to defend themselves. This countertransference response has also been described by Bion in his experience of conducting analytic group therapy for disturbed adults (Bion 1970). During the first year or two of a new therapist's experience with children, there is often a profound sense of having been depleted by the child; this feeling may last for hours or even days after a single session with a particularly disturbed (and disturbing) child. Even in experienced therapists, some children can have this profound effect. Indeed, it is the therapist's openness to this experience, a form of defenselessness, that allows the child's recovery to begin.

In spite of the "bad feelings" involved, the therapist allows the child to put into himself or herself painful feelings or feelings of emptiness (or as Enid Balint says, feelings of being "empty of oneself"), so that the therapist's supportive strengths can act as an ally to the child's beleaguered ego. Winnicott (1965) points out the analyst's dual mentation: she or he remains partly oriented to reality and is partly identified with, even merged with, the child.

I have already alluded to the analogy of the somatic use of transfer factor in the treatment of certain physical illnesses. The key in this analogy is the fact that one person's recovery system can bolster the immune system of another person and can in some cases shift the balance in favor of recovery. The donors of transfer factor, since they are not ill, readily regenerate their own supply, and their immune system is thus weakened only for a transitory period. This parallel has been most clear to me in the examination of the cases of other child therapists, but I do sometimes manage to sense these processes at work within myself, particularly when I have seen a more internally deprived or disorganized child.

The countertransference phenomenon in such cases is of a brief but thoroughly convincing sense of the hopelessness of one's efforts, a kind of depressive coloration amplified by feelings of emptiness, fear, or (often) physical hunger. I do not see this experience as a counteridentification but rather as an aspect of remnant fusion with the child carried on beyond the session. I find myself recovering from this process usually by the next day when, after sleeping, my reparative processes in dreams have acted to restore my own personality organization. Taking account of this effect, I make a practice of scheduling a child who has the most severe depleting effect on me for the last appointment of the day, so that no other children are exposed to me in that state, and vice versa. I also limit the scheduling of children to avoid overlong periods of this degree of emotional exertion. (I actually see, at most, three children consecutively, and usually only two.)

These effects are not limited to the therapy situation. Similar irrational effects can regularly be observed in the supervision of play therapists. As a consultant, one can be aware of a therapist's hopelessness about a child and separately of one's own hopelessness about the therapist's skills—while recognizing that these feelings are paradoxical. They contradict the child's obvious improvement and the therapist's adequate level of competence, of which one remains aware at a more rational analytic level.

Just as the reparative motif, when it occurs, signifies the shift in the child away from domination by bad objects (usually oral, sadomasochistic objects) toward a more balanced system of internal objects, so the emotional tone in supervision reflects the *child's* changed libidinal situation; that is, the emotional flow from the child to the therapist, and in turn to the supervisor, accurately conveys the dominant features of the child's internal object world. Obviously the therapist's own personality colors the transmission, and the play process itself may highlight a different aspect of the child at a particular time. But as a heuristic avenue, the examination of this chain of affective events can often provide a valuable additional source of understanding of the child's communications.

14
Prevalence of
the Reparative Motif

In this chapter, the various threads of the study are drawn together and linked to relevant observations taken from the literature from the early days of psychoanalysis to the present.

In the beginning of the study I set out to examine the theoretical relevance of the reparative motif, a hopeful theme of rescue, reconciliation, or repair, as it emerged in the play themes of children in play therapy. Two children were studied in detail. The historical antecedents of their difficulties, their symptomatic presentation, and the content of their play themes were examined and correlated. The course of recovery of each child was charted through the medium of the thought and fantasy content of each child's play. Corollary criteria of emotional recovery in everyday life were used in support of the hypothetical formulations of the therapeutic process. Some of the determinants of each child's idiosyncratic play themes also were considered.

In order to understand the personality mechanisms involved in the children's play, a model of the personality taken from classical Kleinian theory, modified to serve in the analysis of play themes, was developed.

THE MODEL USED

This model permits both content and organization of play themes to be linked to the model of character structure. Expressive play in the therapeutic context has been regarded as a mirror of the thinking and feeling processes echoing from the depths of the child's mind. Play and dreams are seen as functioning reciprocally, as integrating and expository mechanisms for the child's uncon-

207

scious processes. The changes in the sequential themes in the children's play are used in the study to analyze the personality mechanisms that the children use to improve their emotional resilience.

In the clinical realm, theory and practice have a complementary effect in potentiating the development of clinical knowledge. The results of this study have been applied to extend the theory of reparation beyond its traditional role in the resolution of depressive anxiety. The new formulation emphasizes the role of reparative mechanisms in ensuring the overall coherence of the functioning of the many parts of the child's personality.

THE EVOLVING PLAY THEMES

From the earliest sessions on, children in play therapy begin to approach their central conflicts through a series of successive approximations. The play themes descend in their depravity and intensity to the worst and the most frightening aspects of the child's inner imaginings. Concurrently, the child develops an increasingly supportive relationship with the therapist, which permits this descent to occur. The play acts as a mediator between the children and their fears, and acts as a medium of communication between the child and the therapist.

In the course of the dual relationship (with the play themes and with the therapist), the child develops progressively more effective links between the polarized ("split") aspects of the personality— between terror and delight. This partly cathartic and partly synthetic process has been demonstrated in each of two children who used different play modalities to express their inner worlds of experience.

REPARATION IN PLAY THERAPY

Although the reparative process, like the play process itself, is thought to be largely autochthonous, deriving from some primitive, archetypal will to survive, impairments in the reparative mechanism do occur. Various possibilities have been elaborated for the cause of these impairments. Correspondingly, various aspects of the whole therapeutic experience for the child, the family, and the therapist have been considered as crucial elements in the promotion of the recovery of the reparative mechanisms. Medical analogies, particularly the example of the somatic immune system, have been given to amplify this paradigm of psychological recovery.

The concept of reparation, originally described by Klein, has been extended to include an integrative process which can give coherence to the personality as a whole. The reparative motif in play has been shown to be an advanced form of the young child's use of a cuddly toy or a security blanket as an ally against frightening thoughts or experiences. The reparative mechanism recruits transitional object processes to give the child added security in the face of these inner fears or external threats. Moreover, the mechanism acts to create a fantasy system that tends to neutralize the effect of the perceived danger. In more extensive operation of the reparative mechanism, conflicted areas of the personality (for example, areas in which splitting is prominent) are restructured to minimize the internal stresses.

THEORETICAL FOUNDATIONS

It is worth tracing the thread of psychological thinking that in earlier years has foreshadowed these conclusions. Freud's original studies with Breuer (1895) had led him to formulate the notion of a pathogenic thought or idea (the *idée fixe*) that was causing hysterical problems. He thought of a dissociated part of the self in which the idée fixe and its associated emotions were trapped. Liberation of the *idée fixe* through hypnotic abreaction would remove the hysterical symptoms. Further, he discovered that the connection between symptom and cause might be symbolic, such as healthy people form in dreams. This discovery pointed the way toward recovery through symbolic re-creation and catharsis ("cleansing"). Freud went so far as to suggest that the memories of traumas that have not been sufficiently abreacted are the source of neurotic anxiety. This formulation is consonant with the idea presented in this study of insufficient linking between traumatic foci in the personality and the better-endowed aspects of the personality.

Shapiro and Katz (1978) share Freud's view that "psychoanalysis confirms our recognition of the important place which fairy tales have acquired in the mental life of our children" (p. 281). The work of Shapiro and Katz on the function of fairy tales in the child's ego development shows in a more general context the same trends that I have illustrated in the play stories of individual children.

Bettelheim (1976) also felt that the juxtaposition of loving and vicious themes in fairy tales has a great power to help children to deal with painful conflicts. Fairy tales thus appear to "immunize" children against conflicts by providing a cultural form of expression that is close in content to the children's own fantasy life.

Several authors have elaborated on Klein's formulation of reparation as the mechanism that establishes the reality-testing function of the ego and permits the child to have harmonious relationships. The ability to integrate aggression into a love relationship is felt to be a definitive aspect of mature object relations. Winnicott (1958) perhaps most clearly describes the function of splitting of objects into good and bad domains within the personality. He points out that although splitting eases guilt (about hating the love object), "in payment for this easing, the love loses some of its valuable aggressive component and the hate becomes more disruptive" (p. 207).

Giovacchini (1971) describes the relationship between the ability to create fantasy and the ability to solve the dilemmas presented by character pathology. He shows that fantasy production is an intermediate step between the perception of an inner need and the activation of the proper adjustive techniques to gratify that need. Fantasy is a rehearsal for actual satisfaction. In the two patients he used for illustration, Giovacchini shows that the fantasy lives were either (a) too impoverished or constricted to permit fantasy resolutions of inner conflicts, or (b) so vague and jumbled that the fantasy failed to come together as a cohesive picture, resulting in chaos. As in the progressions seen in the play protocols that I have presented, Giovacchini found that in the course of therapy with adolescent patients, these impoverished or chaotic fantasies gave way to more coherent, predominantly wish-fulfilling fantasies while the disruptive effects of anxiety diminished. In my study I also show both the disruptive and the integrative possibilities of fantasy.

Arlow (1969) addressed the disrupting effects on ordinary functioning of a dominating primitive idea or of a particularly frightening fantasy. It is the neutralizing of the effects of these inner events that permits a return to ordinary functioning.

Enid Balint (1963) points out that it is necessary to be able to keep alive the good objects inside oneself to combat the influence of inner threats and life's realistic threats. If these inner good objects are in imbalance (see Figure 4, Chapter 2), one becomes a helpless victim of all of life's adversities. In her analysis Balint emphasizes the interactivity of the child's fixation and the parents' response. In one of her cases, for example, this interaction led to a void outside and an emptiness inside. Balint confirms the value in treatment of a healthy, affective echo to the child, muted in its intensity but otherwise accurate. In the protocols I have presented, the children designed for themselves a play situation in which they could see and feel this echo through their play and through their effects on me.

Rochlin (1959) studied the role of the prevalent fantasy of imminent abandonment in the creation of emotional problems. In considering the problem of integrating love and hate, he concludes: "There seems to be no final resolution to this conflict" (p. 464). Nevertheless, he shows that the conflict can be sustained within a matrix of balancing mechanisms that render it relatively harmless.

Bloch (1978) showed the complex etiology of many types of childhood fantasy, with particular emphasis on the child's fear of being attacked or killed by the parents. She showed the distorting effects of these fantasies on the child's perception of reality and the therapeutic task of recruiting internal allies in the fight against these persecutory fantasies. More recently, Bloch (1979) has gone further to show the use of fantasy creation as a mechanism with which the child can defend the immature psyche against intolerable assaults. Bloch, one of the few authors to grapple with the problem of how the child recovers in the course of therapy, makes a very important point: the theme the child uses (in my study, the reparative motif) to help defend against frightening fantasies is *itself* transitional. Once developed, it can be discarded, or at least relegated to some "forgotten" part of the child's experience. Bloch presents in detail the play themes of her child patient, and the themes show similar progressions to those presented in this study.

SUMMARY

A detailed study of children's fantasy productions allows the observation of a progression in both the content and the organization of children's play themes. These fantasies can be linked to developmental correlates of the themes of the children's play. A point of discontinuity occurs in the sequence of the play themes when a suddenly more hopeful theme, the reparative motif, emerges. This motif has important implications for the theoretical changes that the child undergoes in the course of psychological recovery.

The Prevalence of the Reparative Motif

Reparative themes are evident in the cases presented in this study and in cases from the literature cited. Nevertheless, it remains to be seen how general the emergence of this theme is in the work of other child therapists, and perhaps in other treatment modalities including the treatment of adults and of families.

The Nature of the Reparative Mechanism

In a more theoretical vein, the reparative motif, and the mechanism that generates it, needs to be better differentiated from defensive fantasies and defense mechanisms. The reparative mechanism is thought of as part of an overall executive organizer of personality functioning, whereas defense mechanisms are more local and specific in their functioning. On the other hand, the entire repertoire of defense mechanisms constitutes a major part of the character structure of an individual. Thus, this differentiation will require a more clear delineation of the place of defense mechanisms in the young child's healthy development.

Factors Disposing Toward Reparation

Since not all children recover in the course of play therapy, and since the clarity of the reparative motif is masked in many children who do recover, some attempt needs to be made to uncover the differentiating features between children who readily produce a reparative motif and others for whom recovery, if it occurs at all, is a long and poorly defined process. Both prognostic signs and the importance of variations in the therapist's technique might emerge from such an investigation.

The Research Challenge

The study of play therapy has, as I mentioned in the preface, suffered from too little attention. Very little research has been conducted into the mechanisms and the events and experiences that occur in play therapy. This is surely in part because of the intrinsic difficulty of describing processes that are themselves revealed only through nondiscursive methods. Our reasoning self has always found the more irrational side of the mind something of a challenge. In children the imaginative faculty is much more profound than in adults. It is therefore even more difficult to categorize it and to make sense of it through ordinary research efforts. But in view of the potentially great rewards, further synthesis of clinical and research-oriented efforts is needed to advance our still quite limited knowledge of the character formation and recovery mechanisms in children in distress.

Tant de chaleur ne peut rester sans effet.

—Michel Tournier, *Gilles et Jeanne*

References

Aichorn, A. (1935). *Neglected Youth.* Glencoe: The Free Press.

Arlow, J. (1969). Unconscious fantasies and disturbances of conscious experience. *Psychoanalytic Quarterly* 38:1-28.

Axline, V. (1947). *Play Therapy.* Boston: Houghton Mifflin.

Balinsky, B. I. (1970). *An Introduction to Embryology.* Philadelphia: Saunders.

Balint, E. (1963). On being empty of oneself. *International Journal of Psycho-Analysis* 44:470-480.

Balint, M. (1952). *Primary Love and Psychoanalytic Technique.* New York: Liveright.

—— (1957). *The Doctor, His Patient and the Illness.* New York: International Universities Press.

—— (1968). *The Basic Fault.* London: Tavistock.

Barker, C. E., and Schmidt, D. (1971). The schizoid problem. *Bulletin of Association of Psychotherapists* 8:35-45.

Bergson, H. (1912). *An Introduction to Metaphysics.* London: Allen and Unwin.

Bernfeld, S. (1929). *Psychology of the Infant.* London: Routledge & Keegan Paul.

Bettelheim, B. (1976). *The Uses of Enchantment.* New York: Alfred Knopf.

Bion, W. (1970). *Experiences in Groups.* New York: Basic Books.

Birtchnell, J. (1970). *A Young Man Preoccupied with His Nose.* Horley, Sussex: Didactic Films.

—— (1973). An analysis of the art productions of a psychiatric patient who was preoccupied with his nose. *American Journal of Art Therapy* 27:201-223.

Bloch, D. (1978). *So the Witch Won't Eat Me.* Boston: Houghton Mifflin.

—— (1979). Birth and death of a defensive fantasy. *Psychoanalytic Review* 66:359-366.

—— (1951). Maternal care and mental health. *Bulletin of the World Health Organization* 3:355-534.

Bowlby, J. (1969). *Attachment.* London: Tavistock.

—— (1973). *Separation.* London: Tavistock.

215

Breen, D. (1975). *The Birth of a First Child*. London: Tavistock.

Cameron, J., Borst, C., Fifer, W., LaVigne, G., and Smith, S. (1972). Remedial reading: A psychoanalytic and operant approach. *British Journal of Medical Psychology* 45:273-278.

Carter, R. (1853). *On the Pathology and Treatment of Hysteria*. London: Cox.

Cooper, S., and Wanerman, L. (1977). *Children in Treatment*. New York: Brunner Mazel.

Dolto, F. (1947). Hypotheses nouvelles concernant les réactions de jalousie à la naissance d'un puiné. *Psyché* 3:7-10.

Ezriel, H. (1950). A psychoanalytic approach to group treatment. *British Journal of Medicial Psychology* 23:59-74.

Fairbairn, W. R. D. (1952). *Psychoanalytic Studies of the Personality*. London: Tavistock.

—— (1954). *An Object Relations Theory of the Personality*. New York: Basic Books.

Ferenczi, S. (1924). On forced phantasies. In *Further Contributions to Psycho-Analysis*. London: Hogarth, 1926.

Foulkes, S. H. (1957). Group analytic dynamics with specific reference to psychoanalytic concepts. *International Journal of Group Psychotherapy* 7:40-52.

Fraiberg, S. H. (1959). *The Magic Years*. New York: Scribners.

Freud, A. (1927). *The Psycho-Analytical Treatment of Children*. London: Imago, 1946.

Freud, S. (1905). Fragment of an analysis of a case of hysteria. *Standard Edition* 7.

—— (1909). Analysis of a five year old boy. *Standard Edition* 10.

—— (1920). Beyond the pleasure principle. *Standard Edition* 18.

Freud, S., and Breuer, J. (1895). On the psychical mechanism of hysterical phenomena. *Standard Edition* 1.

Gardner, R. A. (1971). *Therapeutic Communication with Children*. New York: Science House.

Giovacchini, P. L. (1971). Fantasy formation, ego defect and identity problems. In *Adolescent Psychiatry*, Vol. 1, Eds. S. Feinstein, P. Giovacchini, and D. Miller. New York: Basic Books.

Guntrip, H. (1968). *Schizoid Phenomena, Object Relations and the Self*. London: Hogarth.

Home, H. J. (1971). The problem of resistance as expressed in characteristic transference attitudes. *Bulletin of the Association of Psychotherapists* 8:21-34.

Hug-Hellmuth, H. von (1921). On the technique of child analysis. *International Journal of Psycho-Analysis* 7:84-94.

Isaacs, S. (1933). *Social Development of Young Children.* London: Routledge.

Jones, E. (1948). Introduction to *Contributions to Psychoanalysis, 1921-45.* In: M. Klein, *Envy and Gratitude.* New York: Delta, 1976.

Kalff, D. (1946). *Sand Play.* Glencoe: Free Press.

Khan, M. M. R. (1963). Silence as communication. *Bulletin of the Menninger Clinic* 27:300-313.

—— (1964). Ego distortion, cumulative trauma, and the role of reconstruction in the analytic situation. *International Journal of Psycho-Analysis* 45:272-279.

—— (1969). Les vicissitudes de l'être, du connaitre et de l'éprouver dans la situation analytique. *Bulletin de l'Association Psychanalytique de France* 5:383-393.

Klein, M. (1921). The development of a child. In *Love, Guilt and Reparation and Other Works, 1921-1945.* London: Hogarth, 1975.

—— (1923). Early analysis. In *Love, Guilt and Reparation and Other Works, 1921-1945.* London: Hogarth, 1975.

—— (1926). The psychological principles of early analysis. In *Love, Guilt and Reparation and Other Works, 1921-1945.* London: Hogarth, 1975.

—— (1927). Criminal tendencies in normal children. In *Love, Guilt and Reparation and Other Works, 1921-1945.* London: Hogarth, 1975.

—— (1929a). Personification in the play of children. In *Love, Guilt and Reparation and Other Works, 1921-1945.* London: Hogarth, 1975.

—— (1929b). Infantile anxiety situations reflected in a work of art and in the creative impulse. In *Love, Guilt and Reparation and Other Works, 1921-1945.* London: Hogarth, 1975.

—— (1932). Preface to the first edition. In *Psycho-Analysis of Children.* New York: Delta, 1976.

—— (1934). On criminality. In *Love, Guilt and Reparation and Other Works, 1921-1945.* London: Hogarth, 1975.

—— (1935). A contribution to the psychogenesis of manic-depressive states. In *Love, Guilt and Reparation and Other Works, 1921–1945.* London: Hogarth, 1975.

—— (1937). Love, guilt and reparation. In *Love, Hate and Reparation,* M. Klein and J. Riviere, London: Hogarth, 1937.

—— (1955). The psychoanalytic play technique: its history and significance. In *Envy and Gratitude.* London: Hogarth, 1975.

—— (1957). Envy and gratitude. In *Envy and Gratitude.* London: Hogarth, 1975.

—— (1961). *Narrative of a Child Analysis.* London: Hogarth.

Laing, R. D. (1961). *Self and Others.* London: Tavistock.

Lowenfeld, M. (1935). *Play in Childhood.* London: Gollancz.

—— (1937). A thesis concerning the fundamental structure of the mento-emotional processes in children. *Proceedings of the General Section of the British Psychological Society.*

—— (1938). The world pictures of children: a method of studying and recording them. *British Journal of Medical Psychology* 18:65–101.

—— (1950). The nature and use of the Lowenfeld world technique in work with children and adults. *Journal of Psychology* 30:325–331.

—— (1969). *Brochure of the Institute of Child Psychology.* London: The Institute of Child Psychology.

—— (1979). *The World Technique.* London: Allen and Unwin.

Mackie, R. E. (1969). Intimate and non-intimate relations in therapy. *British Journal of Psychology* 42:371–382.

Mahler, M. S. (1966). Notes on the development of basic moods. In *Psychoanalysis, A General Psychology,* Eds. R. Loewenstein, L. Newman, M. Schur, and A. Solnit. New York: International Universities Press.

The Martha Graham Dance Foundation (1980). *Program Notes.* Performance of The Martha Graham Dance Company, October 18, 1980. Berkeley: Committee for Arts and Lectures, University of California.

Milner, M. (1969). *Hands of the Living God.* London: Hogarth.

Moore, N. (1965). Behaviour therapy in bronchial asthma: A controlled study. *Journal of Psychosomatic Research* 9:257–276.

Moustakas, C. E. (1953). *Psychotherapy with Children.* New York: Harper and Row.

Muller, F. (1864). *Für Darwin.* Leipzig: University Press.

Nagera, U. (1966). The concept of structure and structuralisation, psycho-analytic usage and implications for a theory of learning and creativity. *Psychoanalytic Study of the Child* 22:14–42.

Odent, M. (1976). *Bien Naître*. Paris: Le Seuil.

Rambert, M. (1949). *Children in Conflict*. New York: International Universities Press.

Richards, M. P. M. (1979). *Infancy: World of the Newborn*. New York: Harper and Row.

Rochlin, G. R. (1959). The loss complex: a contribution to the etiology of depression. *Journal of the American Psychoanalytic Association* 7:299–316.

Sechehaye, M. A. (1950). *La Réalisation Symbolique*. New York: International Universities Press.

—— (1956). *A New Psychotherapy in Schizophrenia*, Tr. Grace Rubin-Rabson. New York: Grune & Stratton.

Shapiro, R. B., and Katz, C. L. (1978). Fairy tales, splitting and ego development. *Contemporary Psychoanalysis* 14:591–601.

Smolen, E. M. (1959). Nonverbal aspects of therapy with children. *American Journal of Psychotherapy* 13:872–881.

Stauthamer, J. C. (1982). The first pregnancy: an integrating principle in female psychology. Unpublished Doctoral Dissertation. Berkeley, Ca.: The Wright Institute.

Wax, D. E. (1973). Learning how to pretend: a distinction between intent and pretence observed in the treatment in a borderline psychotic boy. *British Journal of Medical Psychology* 46:297–302.

Wells, H. G. (1912). *Floor Games*. Boston: Small Maynard.

Winnicott, D. W. (1953). Transitional objects and transitional phenomena. *International Journal of Psycho-Analysis* 34:89–97.

—— (1958). *Collected Papers*. London: Tavistock.

—— (1965). *The Maturational Processes and the Facilitating Environment*. London: Hogarth.

—— (1971a). *Therapeutic Consultations in Child Psychiatry*. New York: Basic Books.

—— (1971b). *Playing and Reality*. London: Tavistock.

—— (1977). *The Piggle*. New York: International Universities Press.

Index

Abraham, G., 7
Abraham, K., 15, 45
Adult, therapy with, reparation in, 131–153
Agazarian, Y., 7
Aichorn, A., 15
Analysis
  child, in London, by Klein, 45–47
  of play sessions, 91–99, 113–117
Antibiotic administration 179–180
Antibody creation, 178
Aristotle, 26
Arlow, J., 8, 211
Articulation, content and, of personality, 29–33
Autochthonous thoughts and fantasies, 158, 161–164
Autonomy, reparation as forerunner of, Klein and, 49–51
Axline, V., 20

Balance, of personality, 52–53
Balinsky, B. I., 26
Balint, E., 202, 211
Balint, M., 3, 25, 162, 163, 170
Barker, C. E., 199
Bergson, H., 162, 171
Bernfeld, S., 15
Bettelheim, B., 210
Beyond countertransference, 155–164
Bion, W., 6, 190
Birtchnell, J., on patient's art, 3–4
Bloch, D., 22, 49, 76, 211–212
Boundary phenomena, 31–32
Bower, T. G. R., 1

Bowlby, J., 20–21, 52
Breen, D., 6
Breuer, J., 13, 209
Browning, R., 16
Brutten, M., 7

Cameron, J., 168–169
Carter, R., 13
Change(s)
  in play themes, 123
  reparative, 119–129
Child(ren)
  expressive play of, 59–65, 77–78
  preoccupation of, by conflict, 125–127
Child analysis, in London, by Klein, 45–47
Cleopatra, 193, 195–196
Clinical approach, 55–65
Cohen, S., 6–7
Community, for play therapy, 69
Concept of reparation, 41–54
Conflict(s)
  internal, establishment of, 53–54
  preoccupation of child by, 125–127
Confluence, of danger and love, 122
Conscious responses, 157, 158–160
Constellation, family, reparation in, 181–196
Constitutionally determined emotional dispositions, Klein and, 51–52
Consultation data
  on Christine, 103–104
  on Jennifer, 75–77

Contemporary synthesis, of
theories of play and
development, 21–22
Content, and articulation, of
personality, 29–33
Contrasting technique, 174–175
Contribution, of therapist, 165–180
Cooper, S., 22
Countertransference, 157, 160–161
beyond, 155–164
in play therapy and in play
therapy supervision, 201–203
Course, overall, of play themes, 91–
92
Creation, antibody, 178
Cure, rest, 178–179

Daedalus, 172
Danger, and love, confluence of, 122
Depressive position, onset of,
individuation and, 36–39
Development
of expressive play therapy, 11–22
infant, 20–21
play and, theories of, contemporary synthesis of, 21–22
reflections of, in play themes, 121
Developmental vicissitudes, distorting effects of, 127–129
Diagnostic consultation, 70–72
Direct influences, 169–172
Distance, intimacy and,
therapeutic, 173–174
Distorting effects, of developmental
vicissitudes, 127–129
Dolto, F., 171–172

Early play sessions, analysis of,
93–96

Emergence of reparative motif,
97–99
Emotional dispositions, constitu-
tionally determined, Klein and,
51–52
The Empty Space, 47–48
English school, 25–29
Environment
play, influence of, 170
professional, 200–201
"Errand into the Maze," xv, 192
Establishment of internal conflicts,
53–54
Evans, P., 2
Evolving play themes, 208
Examples, of children's expressive
play, in play therapy, 59–65
Exemplary protocols, 57–59
Expressive play
in play therapy, examples of,
59–65
presuppositions about, 77–78
and symbolism, 19–20
Expressive play technique, of
Lowenfeld, 16–19
Expressive play therapy, develop-
ment of, 11–22
Ezriel, H., 6, 190

Fairbairn, W. R. D., 3, 25, 176
False self, and true, 176
Family constellation, reparation in,
181–196
Fantasies
primitive, revival and sharing of,
173
thoughts and, autochthonous,
158, 161–164
Feldmar, B., 9

Ferenczi, S., 14
Floor Games, 16
Forerunner of autonomy, reparation as, Klein and, 49–51
Foulkes, S. H., 6, 190
Fraiberg, S. H., 21
Freedman, M., 9
Freud, A., 1, 15, 16, 45
Freud, S., 13, 14, 19, 21, 32, 134, 162, 209–210

Gardner, R. A., 174, 175
Gilles et Jeanne, 213
Giovacchini, P. L., 210–211
Giulio Cesare, 193, 195–196
The Martha Graham Dance Company, xv, 192
Green, L., 7
Guntrip H., 3, 171, 176

Haeckel, A., 26
Handel, G. F., 193
Help, from other, 123–124
Hirsch, B., 8
Home, H. J., 14
Hug-Hellmuth, H. von, 14

Icarus, 172
Immune mechanisms, somatic, parallel with, 176–180
Indirect therapeutic influences, 167–169
Individuation, and onset of depressive position, 33–39
Infant development, 20–21
Inferences vis-à-vis reparation, 122–123
Influence(s)
of mind of therapist, 170–172
nonverbal, 169–170

of play environment, 170
therapeutic, indirect and direct, 167–172
Internal conflicts, establishment of, 53–54
Intimacy, and distance, therapeutic, 173–174
Investment, libidinal, of object, 31
Isaacs, S., 25, 52

Jones, E., 15, 45
Jung, C. G., 19, 134

Kalff, D., 19
Katz, C. I., 210
Kernberg, O., 8
Khan, M. M. R., 171, 173, 174
Kjar, R., 47–48
Klein, M., xiii, xiv, 3, 6, 7, 14–15, 16, 18, 19, 20, 21, 53, 76, 122, 133, 134, 150, 161, 189, 207, 209, 210
child analysis in London by, 45–47
and constitutionally determined emotional dispositions, 51–52
earliest ideas of, 43–44
"English school" of, 25–29
first ideas about reparation of, 47–49
and reparation as forerunner of autonomy, 49–51
and splitting and reparation, 51
Kleinian theory, topographical interpretation of, 23–39
Kohut, H., 8

Laing, R. D., 1, 175
Libidinal investment, of object, 31

London, child analysis by Klein in, 45–47
Love, danger and, confluence of, 122
Lowenfeld, M., 6, 52
  expressive play technique of, 16–19
Lowit, I., 6

Mackie, R. E., 4, 162, 171, 172, 174, 200
The Magic Word, 47
Mahler, M. S., 3, 190
Michaelis, K., 47–48
Milner, M., 3
Mind, of therapist, influence of, 170–172
Model, in analysis of play themes, 207–208
Moore, N., 1
Moses, 38
Moustakas, C. E., 20
Movement, psychoanalytic, 13–14
Muller, F., 26

Nagera, U., 21
Nature
  of objects, 29–30
  of reparative mechanism, summary of, 212–213
Nonverbal influences, 169–170

Objects
  nature of, 29–30
  organization of, 30–31
  transitional, 32–33, 34, 35, 36, 37
Occam's razor, 25
Odent, M., 183
Onset of depressive position, individuation and, 33–39

Organization, of objects, 30–31
Other, help from, 123–124
Overall course, of play themes, 91–92

Parallel, with somatic immune mechanisms, 176–180
Pearson, J., 7
Personality
  balance of, 52–53
  content and articulation of, 29–33
Phenomena, boundary, 31–32
The Piggle, 22
Play
  and development, theories of, contemporary synthesis of, 21–22
  expressive, *see* Expressive play
Play environment, influence of, 170
Play scenes, of Christine, 104–113
Play sessions
  analysis of, 91–99, 113–117
  of Jennifer, 78–91
Play technique
  expressive, of Lowenfeld, 16–19
  psychoanalytic, 14–15
Play themes
  changes in, 123
  evolving, 208
  overall course of, 91–92
  reflections of development in, 121
Play therapy
  expressive, 11–22, 59–65
  and play therapy supervision, countertransference in, 201–203
  reparation in, 208–209
Play therapy paradigm, 54
Preoccupation, of child, by conflict, 125–127

Prereparative themes, 96–97

Presuppositions, about expressive play of child, 77–78

Prevalence, of reparative motif, 205–213

Primitive fantasies, revival and sharing of, 173

Princess and the Pea, 38, 126–127

Professional environment, 200–201

Protocols, exemplary, 57–59

Psychoanalytic movement, 13–14

Psychoanalytic play technique, 14–15

Ptolemy, 195

Rambert, M., 19–20

Ravel, M. J., 47

Reflections, of development, in play themes, 121

Regulating mechanisms, transitional, 53

Reimers, S., 2

Reparation
concept of, 41–54
factors disposing towards, summary of, 213
in family constellation, 181–196
as forerunner of autonomy, Klein and, 49–51
inferences vis-à-vis, 122–123
Klein's first ideas about, 47–49
in play therapy, 208–209
splitting and, Klein and, 51
in therapy with adult, 131–153
through transitional processes, 197–203

Reparative change, 119–129

Reparative mechanism(s)
nature of, summary of, 212–213
reparative motif and, 124–125

Reparative motif
emergence of, 97–99
prevalence of, 205–213
and reparative mechanisms, 124–125

Research challenge, 213

Responses, conscious, 157, 158–160

Rest cure, 178–179

Revival, and sharing, of primitive fantasies, 173

Richards, M. P. M., 1, 183

Rochlin, C. R., 3, 211

Ryle, A., 6

Schmidt, D., 200

Sechehaye, M. A., 19, 52

Self, true and false, 176

Setting, for play therapy, 67–72

Shadforth, F., 6

Shapiro, R. B., 210

Sharing, revival and, of primitive fantasies, 173

Sills, J., 2

Singer, M., 1

Skinner, B. F., 1

Smolen, E. M., 20

Somatic immune mechanisms, parallel with, 176–180

Splitting, and reparation, Klein and, 51

Stauthamer, J. C., 186

Supervision, play therapy, countertransference in play therapy and, 201–203

Symbolism, expressive play and, 19–20

Synthesis, contemporary, of theories of play and development, 21–22

Themes
  play, *see* Play themes
  prereparative, 96–97
Theoretical foundations, for
  model, 209–212
Theory(ies)
  Kleinian, topographical inter-
    pretation of, 23–39
  of play and development,
    contemporary synthesis of,
    21–22
Therapeutic influences, indirect,
  167–169
Therapeutic intimacy and distance,
  173–174
Therapist
  contribution of, 165–180
  mind of, influence of, 170–172
Therapy
  with adult, reparation in, 131–153
  play, *see* Play therapy
Thoughts
  and fantasies, autochthonous,
    158, 161–164
  initiated, 157

Topographical interpretation of
  Kleinian theory, 23–39
Tournier, M., 213
Transfer factor, 179
Transitional objects, 32–33, 34, 35,
  36, 37
Transitional processes, reparation
  through, 197–203
Transitional regulating
  mechanisms, 53
True and false self, 176

Vicissitudes, developmental, distorting effects of, 127–129

Wanerman, L., 22
Wax, D. E., 44, 172
Wells, H. G., 16
Winnicott, D. W., 3, 9, 18, 21–22, 25,
  52, 53, 168, 171, 202, 210

Yalom, I. D., 6
Young, R., 7

Zangwill, O., 1